SERIES TEACHING FILM AND MEDIA STUDIES

Teaching Film Censorship and Controversy

Mark Readman

Series Editor: Vivienne Clark
Commissioning Editor: Wendy Earle

British Library Cataloguing-in-Publication Data
A catalogue record for this guide is available from the British Library

ISBN 1 84457 079 7

First published in 2005 by the British Film Institute
21 Stephen Street, London W1T 1LN

Student worksheets to support this guide are supplied at: www.bfi.org.uk/tfms
User name: **filmcens@bfi.org.uk**   Password: **te1908ce**

Design: Amanda Hawkes
Cover photographs: *Irreversible* – courtesy of *bfi* Stills
Printed in Great Britain by: Cromwell Press Ltd

www.bfi.org.uk

The British Film Institute's purpose is to champion moving image culture
in all its richness and diversity across the UK, for the benefit of as wide
an audience as possible, and to create and encourage debate.

Contents

Introduction to the series

Since the introduction of the revised post-16 qualifications (AS and A2 Level) in the UK in September 2000, the number of students taking A Level Film and Media Studies has increased significantly. For example, the latest entry statistics show the following trend:

Subject & Level	June 2001	June 2002	June 2004
A Level Film Studies†	2,017	—	—
AS Level Film Studies	3,852	—	7,996
A2 Level Film Studies	—	2,175	4,161
A Level Media Studies*†	16,293	—	—
AS Level Media Studies*	22,872	—	30,745
A2 Level Media Studies*	—	18,150	22,746

*Three combined awarding bodies' results
† Legacy syllabi – last entry June 2001
(*bfi* Education website – AS/A2 statistics refer to cashed-in entries only)

Inevitably this increase in student numbers has led to a pressing demand for more teachers. But, given the comparatively recent appearance of both subjects at degree level (and limited availability of specialist post-graduate teaching courses), both new and experienced teachers from other disciplines are faced with teaching these subjects for the first time, without a degree-level background to help them with subject content and conceptual understanding. In addition, these specifications saw the arrival of new set topics and areas of study, some of which change frequently, so there is a pressing need for up-to-date resources to help teacher preparation, as well as continuing professional development courses.

I meet a large number of Film and Media Studies teachers every year in the course of my various roles and developed the concept and format of this series with the above factors, and busy and enthusiastic teachers, in mind. Each title provides an accessible reference resource, with essential topic content, as well as clear guidance on good classroom practice to improve the quality of teaching and students' learning. We are confident that, as well as supporting the teacher new to these subjects, the series provides the experienced specialist with new critical perspectives and teaching approaches as well as useful content.

The two sample schemes of work included in Section 1 are intended as practical models to help get teachers started. They are not prescriptive, as any working scheme of work has to be developed with the specific requirements of an assessment context, and ability of the teaching group, in mind. Likewise, the worksheets provided in the online materials offer examples of good practice, which can be adapted to your specific needs and contexts. In some cases, the online resources include additional resources, such as interviews and illustrative material, available as webnotes. See www.bfi.org.uk/tfms.

The series is clear evidence of the range, depth and breadth of teacher expertise and specialist knowledge required at A Level in these subjects. Also, it is an affirmation of why this subject area is such an important, rich and compelling one for increasing numbers of 16- to 19-year-old students. Many of the more theoretical titles in the series include reference to practical exercises involving media production skills. It is important that it is understood here that the current A Levels in Media and Film Studies are not designed as vocational, or pre-vocational, qualifications. In these contexts, the place of practical media production is to offer students active, creative and engaging ways in which to explore theory and reflect on their own practice.

It has been very gratifying to see that the first titles in this series have found an international audience, in the USA, Canada and Australia, among others, and we hope that future titles continue to be of interest in international moving image education.

Every author in the series is an experienced practitioner of Film and/or Media Studies at this level and many have examining/moderating experience. It has been a pleasure to work closely with such a diverse range of committed professionals and I should like to thank them for their individual contributions to this expanding series.

Vivienne Clark
Series Editor
September 2005

● Key features

● Assessment contexts for the major UK post-16 Film and Media Studies specifications
● Suggested schemes of work
● Historical contexts (where appropriate)
● Key facts, statistics and terms
● Detailed reference to the key concepts of Film and Media Studies
● Detailed case studies
● Glossaries
● Bibliographies
● Student worksheets, activities and resources (available online) – ready for you to print and photocopy for the classroom.

● Other titles available in the series include:

● *Teaching Scriptwriting, Screenplays and Storyboards for Film & TV Production* – Mark Readman
● *Teaching TV Sitcom* – James Baker
● *Teaching Digital Video Production* – Pete Fraser and Barney Oram
● *Teaching TV News* – Eileen Lewis
● *Teaching Women and Film* – Sarah Gilligan
● *Teaching World Cinema* – Kate Gamm
● *Teaching TV Soaps* – Lou Alexander and Alison Cousens
● *Teaching Contemporary British Broadcasting* – Rachel Viney
● *Teaching Contemporary British Cinema* – Sarah Casey Benyahia
● *Teaching Music Video* – Pete Fraser
● *Teaching Auteur Study* – David Wharton and Jeremy Grant
● *Teaching Men and Film* – Matthew Hall
● *Teaching Analysis of Film Language* – David Wharton and Jeremy Grant.

● Forthcoming titles include:

Teaching Video Games; Teaching Stars and Performance; Teaching TV Drama; Teaching Short Films.

SERIES EDITOR: Vivienne Clark is a former Head of Film and Media Studies and an Advanced Skills Teacher. She is currently an Associate Tutor of *bfi* Education and Principal Examiner for A Level Media Studies for one of the English awarding bodies. She is a freelance teacher trainer, media consultant and writer/editor, with several published textbooks and resources, including *GCSE Media Studies* (Longman 2002), *Key Concepts & Skills for Media Studies* (Hodder Arnold 2002). She is also a course tutor for the *bfi*/Middlesex University MA Level module, An Introduction to Media Education, and a link tutor and visiting lecturer for the Central School of Speech & Drama PGCE (Media with English), London.

AUTHOR: Mark Readman is a Programme Manager and Advanced Practitioner at Bridgwater College in Somerset. He is an Assessor and External Verifier respectively for two of the English awarding bodies and a member of the South West Screen Script Readers' Bank. He is also the author of *Teaching Scriptwriting, Screenplays and Storyboards for Film & TV Production* in this series.

Introduction

Assessment contexts

Awarding body & level	Subject	Unit code	Module/Topic
✓ AQA AS Level	Media Studies	Med2	Textual Topics in Contemporary Media
✓ AQA A2 Level	Media Studies	Med4	Texts and Contexts in the Media
✓ OCR A2 Level	Media Studies	2735	Media Issues and Debates
✓ WJEC A2 Level	Film Studies	FS6	Critical Studies
✓ SQA Advanced Higher	Media Studies	DF14	Media Analysis
✓ CCEA A2 Level	Moving Image Arts		Exploring and Experimenting with Forms & Styles
✓ EdExcel BTEC Nationals	Media	1	Understanding the Media
✓ EdExcel BTEC Nationals	Media	37	Film Studies

This guide is also relevant to the following specifications, as well as to international and Lifelong Learning courses:

- AQA, EdExcel, OCR – GNVQ and AVCE media and communication.

Other guides in this series offer excellent complementary information to this guide:

- *Teaching World Cinema* – Kate Gamm
- *Teaching Women and Film* – Sarah Gilligan
- *Teaching Men and Film* – Matthew Hall
- *Teaching Auteur Study* – David Wharton and Jeremy Grant
- *Teaching Analysis of Film Language* – David Wharton and Jeremy Grant.

Other *bfi* resources which support this topic include:

- C Dupin and I O'Sullivan, 1999, *Censorship: A 16+ Guide* (www.bfi.org.uk/nationallibrary/collections/16+/censorship/)
- R Falcon, 1994, *Classified!: A Teacher's Guide to Film and Video Censorship and Classification*, bfi
- Screenonline (www.screenonline.org.uk).

● Specification links

The study of censorship, shocking cinema and controversy outlined in this guide is relevant to the following specification areas:

AQA AS Media Studies Module 2: Textual Topics in Contemporary Media
Film and Broadcast Fiction:
- Debates around meaning and evaluation
- Issues of audience
- Issues of representation
- Questions of and debates around values and ideology

British Newspapers:
- Analysis and evaluation of press coverage of an issue or story
- Press ideologies

AQA A2 Media Studies Module 4: Texts and Contexts in the Media
The Production and Manufacture of News:
- Balance and bias in the news

Representations:
- General issues of representation and stereotyping within the media
- Representation and power in the media

Media Audiences:
- Theories of audience. How audiences read media texts.
- Influence of new technologies on media–audience relations

OCR A2 Media Studies Unit 2735: Media Issues and Debates
- Censorship and film

WJEC A2 Film Studies Unit FS6: Critical Studies
- Shocking cinema
- Regulation and censorship

CCEA A2 Moving Image Arts: Exploring and Experimenting with Forms and Styles
- Alternative approaches – arthouse and avant-garde work

EdExcel BTEC National Diploma/Certificate in Media Unit 1: Understanding the Media
- Representation – legal and ethical issues

EdExcel BTEC National Diploma in Media Unit 37: Film Studies

- Issues and debates (censorship)
- Film audiences

Rationale: Why teach film censorship and controversy?

A couple of examples:

- In the early 1980s a teenager, after obsessively watching *Brideshead Revisited* (ITV, 1981) on television, embarks on a reckless buying spree of vintage clothing in order to emulate the characters portrayed by Jeremy Irons and Anthony Andrews.
- In 2003 a teenager, after obsessively watching *The Matrix* (Andy Wachowski/Larry Wachowski, USA/Australia, 1999) on DVD, embarks on a reckless killing spree, murdering his family.

What's the difference between these two tragic cases? Well, only in the first one is there a provable link between the media text and a specific effect; reader, I was that teenager. Even here the 'effect' was not simply a result of a 'message' being projected by the text, but an active interpretation of aspects of it that was subsequently incorporated into an ideological framework, which included aspirations of class, education and taste, and then translated into (non-violent) behaviour.

This may seem like a flippant way to introduce a serious subject, but it addresses an issue at the heart of the debate, namely the degree to which negative effects – harm, trauma, imitation – can be ascribed to media products. If they cannot, then the notion of cutting and banning controversial media material becomes, at least, questionable.

This guide is principally concerned with studying debates surrounding UK film censorship and related controversies, but it also examines the topic of shocking cinema, which focuses on the creation and effects of 'shock' (with various definitions) on the spectator. The schemes of work, case studies and worksheets aim to support the study of these related topics.

From a teaching perspective, it is useful to acknowledge the difficulties from the outset. As teachers, we may be worried by ethical issues – is it justifiable for us to show and discuss material which learners may find unpleasant and disturbing? There are professional issues: What's our legal situation? Should we inform parents? There are personal issues – we may feel uncomfortable discussing controversial texts. There are intellectual issues – the questions are complex and there are no definitive answers, so is it a feasible project for the classroom? There are practical issues – so much has been written and said on the subject in different forms that it may be impossible to cover it.

Despite all of these legitimate reservations and objections, studying censorship can be stimulating, challenging and rewarding. This is not least because it is a cross-disciplinary subject. From a Media/Film Studies perspective, it involves decoding texts, negotiating signs and contesting meanings; from a sociological perspective, it is about examining the function of censorship and the social assumptions on which it is based; from a psychological perspective, the focus is on the impact of filmic representations on the individual psyche; from a philosophical perspective, questions might be asked about the nature of liberty and the meaning of shock; from a political perspective, the emphasis is on the formation of policy, its execution and a consideration of the interests served by it; and from a legal perspective, it might be approached by ascertaining the degree to which an actual offence can be proved.

The resonance of the subject within these different fields gives it a significance that goes beyond many Media and Film Studies topics and consequently, its capacity to engage can be much greater and wider. In addition to the debates around content, the study of censorship can be an excellent training ground for critical thinking – logic, deductive and inductive methods, empirical enquiry and syllogistic reasoning can all be practised and tested during such a course. It also provides an opportunity to critique popular discourses around the subject – the invocations of 'science', the mobilisation of apocalyptic tropes and the determinants on journalistic practice.

In summary then, there are some very good reasons for teaching about film censorship and controversy:

- It can increase the sophistication of learners' media literacy regarding issues of address, identification, genre and representation.
- It can develop an appreciation of the importance of context when decoding texts and an understanding of the responses of audiences and other institutions.
- It can open up ethical debates around liberty, democracy, paternalism and citizenship.
- It can develop an understanding of the discourses and journalistic practices which surround controversial texts.
- It can improve critical thinking, encouraging learners to question assumptions about texts, effects and audiences and to test the validity of arguments.

Finally, one could argue that in an age when extreme images are available through channels that cannot effectively be policed, it is crucial for issues of accessibility, freedom of expression, and the potential for personal and social harm to be assessed dispassionately, responsibly and with intellectual rigour. This guide is intended to offer some ways of doing this.

● Key debates

The following are the main issues and debates that students are likely to be required to study and respond to in their examination answers:

Film censorship

- What are the motives for film censorship?
- What assumptions is it based upon?
- Whose interests does it serve?
- How is censorship culturally and historically specific?
- Is censorship a legitimate activity in a democracy?

Controversy and the press

- What are moral panics?
- How are they instigated and fuelled by the media?
- What factors might motivate the scapegoating of films?

Shocking cinema

- What is 'shock' in film?
- What different types of shock exist?
- To what extent is shock dependent upon the intersection of a range of cultural and textual factors?

How to use this guide

This guide is divided into three sections. In Section 1, there are two schemes of work – one addressing censorship, one addressing the concept of shock. Each scheme suggests areas that might be covered on a week-by-week basis and ties activities to the worksheets that are available as online resources. The schemes are not, of course, prescriptive and, although some attempt has been made to produce a logical order, the different areas could be delivered out of this sequence and some missed out altogether. Section 2 is built around key areas that comprise the subject of censorship and controversy, such as the work of the BBFC (British Board of Film Classification), sex, violence and the nature of shock. Each area includes information, examples and suggestions for teaching and student activities. Section 3 contains case studies – discussions of significant films and their relevance to the subject, and an example of a critical debate between two well-known figures in this field, Aminatta Forna and Mark Kermode.

In addition, there are some webnotes containing important pieces of legislation, an interview with a senior BBFC examiner, Pete Johnson, BBFC press releases too lengthy to include in the body of the guide, some sample exam questions and a sample letter for use with parents, as well as some student notes with extract materials to accompany some of the worksheets. The worksheets referenced in the sample schemes of work are available at: **www.bfi.org.uk/tfms**. To access the pages, enter **username: filmcens@bfi.org.uk** and **password: te1908ce**. If you have any problems please email: education.resources@bfi.org.uk.

Approaches to teaching

The material under investigation here is, by definition, potentially controversial and shocking and therefore needs to be handled carefully in the classroom. It's a good idea to be explicit about your aims and to avoid surprises. Being explicit means ensuring that your students, their parents (if appropriate) and your institution know what you are doing and why you are doing it. Avoiding surprises means not showing something to students without carefully priming them about the content, duration and reasons for watching it. This kind of preparatory work should ensure that students approach the topic with a more mature and reflective mindset, as opposed to the defensive bravado which can sometimes arise. For the same reason it is a good idea to encourage students to depersonalise their responses. This involves setting up activities and posing questions which make it difficult for responses to relate to their own supposed resilience and experience, but which instead encourage informed speculative responses about how a particular age group or interest group might respond to a text and why. Useful in this context are role-play exercises, which have the additional benefit of requiring students to research the position that they are supposed to be advocating (even if this takes the form of a letter to the BBFC from a 'concerned parent' arguing that a particular film's certificate is too low – a simple but effective exercise). Showing carefully selected extracts from appropriate films, setting up small group activities and then collating responses with the whole group can sometimes make it easier to monitor and guide the type and level of critical engagement which takes place.

You can even make a virtue out of this 'self-regulatory practice' by discussing your agenda and decision-making processes with the students. Similarly you can take the opportunity to address the significance of the classroom as a viewing environment which has specific conditions of reception; students could be led to acknowledge that the formal requirements of the classroom, together with the regulatory presence of the teacher, might make viewing certain kinds of material more shocking or more uncomfortable than if they were able to determine the environment and company themselves. How, also, might responses be determined by viewing with a mixed or single-sex audience? These discussions do, of course, elicit a personal response and therefore need to be tailored to the group(s) you're working with.

Decisions about what to show, what not to show and how to generate effective work are ultimately made according to specific circumstances. It is quite possible to do work on the issues around representations of sexual violence by reading film reviews, critical essays and BBFC reports or to do work on representations of violence by examining films on the 12/12A and 15 thresholds. It is the critical approach which is paramount and this will be engendered most successfully if aims are clear, communication is inclusive and activities are geared to specific groups of learners.

Schemes of work

These schemes of work are intended to generate understanding of some key concepts relating to film censorship, controversy and shocking cinema and to provide opportunities from the outset of applying them to texts and concrete examples. A key aim is that students should acquire concepts, perspectives and approaches which can then be tested and implemented, rather than simply acquiring a body of knowledge.

● Scheme of work 1: Film censorship

Aims:
To understand
- The concepts of censorship and classification
- The ways in which these are determined and implemented
- The ways in which research and reporting can create controversy
- Factors determining valid research

Outcomes:
- Evaluation and application of BBFC Guidelines
- Analysis of 'violence' on screen
- Analysis of the rhetoric of effects and research methods
- The development of research tools

Week 1 The concept of censorship
The BBFC – legal status, guidelines, age classification **Worksheet 7**

Week 2 Violence – BBFC concerns, meanings of violence **Worksheet 2**
Analysis of examples **Worksheets 1** and **2**
Realism **Worksheet 4**

Week 3 Sexual violence – *Straw Dogs* **Worksheet 9**

Week 4 Censorship agenda – class **Worksheet 10**
Moral panics – journalistic rhetoric **Worksheet 8**
Summary – Forna vs Kermode **Worksheet 16**

Week 5 The effects model **Worksheet 5**
Research methods **Worksheet 6**

Week 6 Carrying out research

● Scheme of work 2: Shocking cinema

Aims:

To understand

- Ways of identifying the nature of shock, different types of shock and its generation through textual and contextual factors
- Ways of understanding the nature of shock in a historical/cultural context

Outcomes:

- Analysis of different types of 'shocking' events on screen
- Analysis of 'shocking' events from other periods and relation to context

Week 1 The concept of shock **Worksheet 11**
Analysis of examples

Week 2 Graphic shock – *Un Chien andalou* **Worksheet 12**
Analysis of other examples

Week 3 Narrative and textual shock
Psycho, *Spooks*
Nomination of comparable examples

Week 4 Surprise vs shock **Worksheet 13**
Analysis of examples

Week 5 Ideological/cultural/historical factors **Worksheet 14**
Identifying matrix of factors in relation to examples **Worksheet 15**

Week 6 Designing and carrying out audience research into the phenomenon
Worksheet 6

● Research and resources

The films and other texts referred to are by no means prescriptive. The films can be acquired fairly easily but you could substitute your own appropriate examples. The television programmes referred to may be harder to acquire, but the summaries and transcripts in the body of this guide may suffice. Articles from *The Guardian* can be obtained online (www.guardianunlimited.co.uk); BBFC press releases, which are a mine of valuable information on the decision-making processes at the Board, can be found at www.bbfc.co.uk; and some articles from *Sight and Sound* may also be obtained online (http://www.bfi.org.uk/sightandsound): the archive is limited and selective so back issues or library copies are an alternative.

2

Background

Timeline (British context)

1909   The Cinematograph Act introduced. This gives local authorities the power to grant or withhold licences from cinemas, ostensibly on the grounds of fire safety, but it also confers discretionary powers upon councils to implement taste and decency criteria.

1912   The British Board of Film Censors (BBFC) established by the film industry in conjunction with the Home Office, in response to local authorities imposing their own widely varying standards of censorship. The aim is to bring a degree of uniformity to those standards. There are only two 'rules': no portrayal of Christ and no nudity.

1916   T P O' Connor appointed President of the BBFC. He summarises Board policy by drawing up a list of 43 grounds for deletion, which include 'the irreverent treatment of sacred objects', 'realistic horrors of warfare' and 'men and women in bed together'.

1923   The Home Office recommends that all local authorities adopt the practice of London and Middlesex County Councils, which is to only allow cinemas to show BBFC-certificated films.

1926   *The Battleship Potemkin* (Sergei Eisenstein, USSR, 1925) is banned by the BBFC, ostensibly on the grounds of 'violence', but there may be a political motive as the General Strike has recently ended in the UK. It is not granted a certificate until 1954.

1932   The advisory 'H' certificate is introduced in order to indicate a horror theme and unsuitability for children.

1952   The Cinematograph Act revises the certification system to institute a category to exclude children: the 'X' certificate is introduced for over 16s only.

1954   *The Wild One* (Laslo Benedek, USA, 1953) is refused a certificate by the BBFC amid concerns about juvenile crime. It is not awarded a certificate until 1967.

1959   The Obscene Publications Act is passed.

1960   D H Lawrence's 1928 novel, *Lady Chatterley's Lover*, is successfully defended against the Obscene Publications Act, making it freely available for the first time since its publication.

1965   Mary Whitehouse founds the National Viewers' and Listeners' Association.

1970   The age limit for the 'X' category is raised from 16 to 18.

1971   *A Clockwork Orange* is released and press reports about supposed 'copycat' acts of violence follow. In 1973 its director Stanley Kubrick withdraws the film in the UK.

1974   *The Exorcist* (William Friedkin, USA, 1974) is released.

1975   Ex-independent filmmaker James Ferman becomes Secretary of the BBFC. He dominates film censorship in Britain for the next 24 years.

1982   The 'PG', '15', '18' and 'R18' categories are introduced.

1984   The Video Recordings Act is passed, after a press-fuelled moral panic about 'video nasties', making it an offence for videos to be sold or hired unless they have a certificate from the BBFC. The name is changed to the British Board of Film Classification.

1987   Random shootings in Hungerford are linked in the press with the first two *Rambo* films, although there is no evidence that the killer, Michael Ryan, saw either of them.

1989   The '12' certificate is introduced.

1993   Two-year-old Liverpool child James Bulger is killed by two older boys. The press claims that the killers were influenced by the horror film *Child's Play 3* (Jack Bender, USA, 1991), although the subsequent investigation fails to prove that they have even seen the film.

1994   The Amendment to the Video Recordings Act is passed in the wake of the Bulger killing and the Newson Report on the supposed effects of screen violence. This includes a clause covering potential harm caused to viewers and forces the BBFC to apply much stricter criteria to video classification.

1996   David Cronenberg's *Crash* (Canada, 1996) is screened at the London Film Festival. Despite a sustained campaign against the film by *The Evening Standard* and *The Daily Mail*, *Crash* is given an uncut 18 certificate in 1997. Westminster Council bans it.

1999   Robin Duval, ex-Deputy Director of Programmes at the Independent Television Commission, takes over as Director of the BBFC when James Ferman retires.

2002   '12' certificate for cinemas is replaced with the advisory '12A' certificate.

2003   Ofcom set up.

2004   David Cooke, ex-Associate Political Director at the Northern Ireland Office, takes over as BBFC Director.

Institutions and regulation: The BBFC

The British Board of Film Classification is the body responsible for classifying films, videos, DVDs and digital games in the UK. It is an independent, non-governmental body funded via the fees it charges to those who submit work for classification. It applies age-restrictive classifications and, if necessary, recommends cutting or otherwise altering a film in order to make it conform to their guidelines. It may not pass any material likely to infringe the criminal law.

The BBFC has complete control (and statutory responsibilities) over video classification and censorship, but has less power regarding theatrical releases; it classifies films on behalf of local authorities, but local authorities still have the power to reject a BBFC decision about a particular film. For example when Sam Raimi's *Spider-Man* (USA, 2002) was released with a '12' certificate, despite having been heavily marketed to children via toys and cereal,

> Many local authorities – responding to appeals by cinema owners, in turn besieged by parental victims of pester power – overruled the BBFC classification with a PG rating that permitted children to see it. (Kennedy, 2002)

The process of classification involves a film being submitted by a distributor with a stated certificate request, then being viewed and assessed against particular criteria and a certification decision reached (these criteria, the BBFC guidelines, are available from www.bbfc.co.uk). The BBFC's decisions must have particular regard to the law, specifically the Obscene Publications Act, the Protection of Children Act and the Criminal Justice Act; its decisions (and therefore the reason for its existence) would become insupportable if they were subsequently overturned by legal actions.

The 1959 Obscene Publications Act (OPA) (see notes on this at www.bfi.org.uk/tfms) defines obscenity as something which must 'tend to deprave and corrupt' but exempts work with artistic or educational merit. Although originally only intended to cover literature, a 1977 amendment included film – an amendment which had been lobbied for by James Ferman, the then Secretary of the BBFC, in order to legitimise his defence of 'serious' films. The Act's rather old-fashioned-sounding phrasing must still be taken seriously by the Board as it is charged with the responsibility for ensuring that such material is not made publicly available.

The 1978 Protection of Children Act (see notes on this at www.bfi.org.uk/tfms) makes it an offence to distribute, show and possess 'indecent' photographs (including films) of children under the age of 16. Unlike the OPA, it does not exempt works with supposed artistic merit. The act seems to have been driven by concerns about child pornography and, since 1994, also outlaws 'doctored' images. The result for the BBFC is that it must pay a great deal of attention to anything which could be interpreted as a recording of an indecent act involving an actual child. In this sense it is similar to the 1937 Cinematograph Films (Animals) Act, which makes it an offence to distribute or exhibit a film whose creation involved actual cruelty to an animal.

> To access online materials go to *Teaching Film Censorship and Controversy* at **www.bfi.org.uk/tfms** and enter User name: **filmcens@bfi.org.uk** and Password: **te1908ce**.

The BBFC's history (described in detail in Dewe Matthews, 1994) can be seen as a series of expedient moves, responses to political pressure and attempts to deal with new technologies and shifting social attitudes, all of which can be highlighted by examining key moments. One brief example is the introduction of a demanding set of statutory obligations under the 1984 Video Recordings Act (see notes on this at www.bfi.org.uk/tfms) – a piece of legislation driven by the 'video nasties' scare in the early 1980s. Apparently a key piece of wording in the act was determined by the dogged insistence of moral campaigner Mary Whitehouse that video classification must have 'special regard to the likelihood of video works ... being viewed in the family home', a clause which James Ferman admitted later was unenforceable (Dewe Matthews, 1994, p246). This wording, however, provides a justification for cutting some things out of videos which were passed in the cinema version of the same film. Another justification for this is that scenes can be viewed out of context, played in slow motion and freeze-framed, although, as Nigel Andrews argues

> The repetition facility in video – the fact that you can rewind and re-watch a scene again and again – works to reduce, not to increase, a film's shock value. Repetition not only creates the contempt bred of familiarity but it helps to expose ... the technical artifices that create the horrific effect. It's probably the healthiest attribute that video has. (1984, p47)

The history of how censorship and classification evolved in the UK can reveal some of the assumptions and fears that underlay the decisions and policies that resulted. A historical perspective in the classroom can provide some useful ways in to the subject as it can highlight the fact that censorship is always historically and culturally specific and that interpretations of texts and responses to them will always be (and can be demonstrated to be) subject to revision in the future. We can witness some of this process of revision happening now as the BBFC removes its prohibition on different DVD versions of the same film circulating with different certificates; it is now willing to classify 'special editions', uncut versions and 'directors' cuts' of films previously classified on video/DVD providing the title and packaging distinguishes it from the earlier version.

The bulk of the BBFC's work today may well be, as Barker *et al* (2001) suggest, 'routinist and almost mechanical: helping distributors to fit films within the "windows" of the various classifications' by, for example, identifying cuts that need to made in order for a film to be passed at '15' for the cinema and which additional cuts may be necessary in order to give it the same certificate on video. Nevertheless, the history-by-worst-case approach has the advantage of often providing us with the exposure of hidden agendas when decisions are challenged and the machinery of censorship is subjected to scrutiny.

Some key themes emerge in the history of censorship, many of which still obtain today. Tom Dewe Matthews argues that

> ... the practice of censorship as a means of blanking out what we do not want to witness has not been an arbitrary vendetta against precocious voices. It is, in fact, a systematic process which chooses its victims with care. The direction and intensity of censorship is determined by the popularity of a new medium. Thus film was censored in Britain more than any of the other media until cinema was superseded by television as the primary mass medium in the fifties. (1994, p1)

There is not space here to give a detailed historical account (Dewe Matthews' book does this comprehensively up to 1994), but there is an attempt to identify the key themes and issues relevant to censorship. Some of these themes and issues have been and are explicitly stated by the BBFC, politicians and moral campaigners; others are more implicit and the assumptions that underpin them can be teased out and argued about. They revolve around content which is variously seen as shocking, corrupting, disturbing or an incitement to criminal activity, and fundamentally depend upon a notion of the power of the moving image to produce influence and effects. There is inevitably overlap between some of the categories described below, but a degree of separation is useful for teaching purposes.

Key themes: Controversial issues, causes for concern and motives for censorship

The following have emerged as key themes and issues in relation to film censorship, controversy and shocking cinema:

- Violence
  - graphic representation and realism
  - audience effects models and alternatives
- Corrupting the young
- Controversy and the press
- Sex and nudity
- Sexual violence
- Religion
- Class
- Language
- Shock

These points are discussed in some detail in the rest of this section of the book, except for language, which is covered in detail in Case study 3.

● Violence

This is a major area for concern for the BBFC, essentially due to a supposed relationship between violence on screen and violence in the real world. Its classification guidelines outline the general ethos:

> In making decisions, our concerns include
> - Portrayal of violence as a normal solution to problems
> - Heroes who inflict pain and injury
> - Callousness towards victims
> - Encouraging aggressive attitudes
> - Taking pleasure in pain or humiliation
>
> Works which glorify or glamorise violence will receive a more restrictive classification and may even be cut. (BBFC classification guidelines)

Although we may agree that these are valid concerns, applying them and making subsequent decisions is clearly not a straightforward activity. A way of highlighting this problem with students is to screen something fairly innocuous and ask them to identify examples of the BBFC's concerns regarding violence. An example could be an extract from the James Bond film *The Spy Who Loved Me* (Lewis Gilbert, UK, 1977) in which Roger Moore's Bond vanquishes 'Jaws' in a railway carriage by electrocuting him and propelling him through a window, makes a joke about it and then falls into the arms of Barbara Bach for a sexual reward. Students are likely to find examples of all of the BBFC's concerns.

Worksheet 1 sets up this activity and then takes the next step by asking for a decision about classification and/or cutting to meet a particular classification. Students are unlikely to feel that the violence in a James Bond film is anything to be concerned about. This is despite the fact that violence is often portrayed as an inevitable solution to a problem, our hero routinely inflicts pain and injury on his adversaries, often expressing his pleasure and callousness at this in the form of a witticism, and we are encouraged to celebrate Bond's violent victories. The points that should arise are that:

● 'Violence' on screen is not a single quantifiable entity, but something which is meaningful because of its portrayal and its contextualisation within a narrative.
● The identification of 'violence' on screen is always an act of interpretation.

1 of 2 pages

To access student worksheets and other online materials go to *Teaching Film Censorship and Controversy* at **www.bfi.org.uk/tfms** and enter User name: **filmcens@bfi.org.uk** and Password: **te1908ce**.

Examples of the BBFC's concerns regarding violence being put into practice can be found in the 'Press Releases' section of its website where we can find this response to the film *Fight Club* (David Fincher, USA, 1999):

> This film has been classified '18' for cinema release to adult audiences, after cuts.

> Concerns have been raised in advance of the film's public release in Britain about its violent content, the encouragement it may give to the illegal sport of bare-knuckle fighting, and what has been perceived as its generally 'antisocial' effect.

The violent content of *Fight Club* is rather less than the many other films which have passed entirely without public or media concern. In particular, the scenes of fighting occupy only a small part of overall screen time. Therefore, audiences who expect a large quantity of fist fighting and graphic violence are likely to be disappointed. Nevertheless, there are two scenes in which the Board judged that the violence was excessively sustained and in conflict with the concern expressed in the BBFC Guidelines about taking pleasure in pain or sadism. In both scenes there was an indulgence in the excitement of beating a defenceless man's face into a pulp. The Board required that cuts be made in each case.

The Board has also looked very closely at other elements which might be thought to provide dangerously instructive information or to encourage anti-social behaviour. Such 'instructional detail' as there is is either misleading or unlikely to be harmful to an individual or society.

The film as a whole is – quite clearly – critical and sharply parodic of the amateur fascism which in part it portrays. Its central theme of male machismo (and the antisocial behaviour that flows from it) is emphatically rejected by the central character in the concluding reels.

The Board recognizes that there will be arguments on both sides about the merits or possible effects of the film, but is satisfied that, in its classified form, *Fight Club* will be enjoyed by a great many viewers without harm either to themselves or to anyone else.

(www.bbfc.co.uk, Press Releases, 6 December, 1999)

There are some assumptions here, underpinning a decision to cut a film for an adult audience, which need examining:

- There is a line that can be drawn in a representation of fictional violence beyond which it is possible to describe it as 'excessive'.
- This portrayal of violence may in some way be harmful or damaging to some viewers.

Both of these assumptions are problematic. The first is inevitably a matter of interpretation – some viewers will have different thresholds, different levels of competence and experience with media texts, and different understandings of what constitutes violence on screen – a notion of the 'reading' process explored in detail by Annette Hill (1997) and discussed below (see p35–7). The second is difficult, if not impossible to prove. Martin Barker's work is particularly useful at this point as it asks some radical questions about this thing called 'media violence', about which so much concern has been expressed and so much policy formulated:

The expression 'media violence' has to be one of the most commonly repeated, and one of the most ill-informed, of all time. It is supposed to encompass everything from cartoons (ten-ton blocks dropped on Tom's head by Jerry, Wily Coyote plummeting down yet another mile-deep canyon); children's action adventure films (the dinosaurs of *Jurassic Park* alongside playground scuffles in *Grange Hill* and last-reel shootouts in westerns); news footage from Rwanda and Bosnia; documentary footage showing the police attacking Rodney King in Los Angeles; horror films from Hammer to cult gore movies; the range from Clint Eastwood as the voiceless hard man of *Dirty Harry* to Arnie as the violent humorist in almost any of his films, etc etc.

And therein lies the point: no single ground has ever been given for us to suppose that such a list has any single property in common other than that certain critics don't like them. It is a useless conflation of wholly different things. Yet somehow that conflation endlessly continues. And whenever the phrase 'media violence' is used it conjures up one image above all else: an image of motiveless mayhem, to which words such as 'gratuitous' easily attach themselves. (1997, p27)

Worksheet 2 asks students to count the number of violent acts on the tape and to complete a table with a brief description of each act. The follow-up questions are designed to demonstrate that this exercise offers little in the way of understanding of the meanings of the events on screen and that a simplistic quantitative analysis of a media text may not be valuable in reaching an understanding of its meanings.

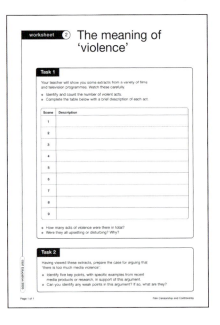

To access student worksheets and other online materials go to *Teaching Film Censorship and Controversy* at **www.bfi.org.uk/tfms** and enter User name: **filmcens@bfi.org.uk** and Password: **te1908ce**.

What should emerge here is the idea that 'violence' is not something that can be taken out of context and that the genre of the text, the contextualisation of the action within a narrative, the nature of its representation and the ways in which audiences might understand and interpret something as 'violent' all need to be taken into account.

Mark Kermode addresses exactly this point in his discussion of the controversy surrounding *The Evil Dead* (Sam Raimi, USA, 1981):

> *The Evil Dead* scored a major hit with fans, but ran into trouble with British censors. In UK cinemas, the movie was cut by forty seconds by the British Board of Film Classification, who recognised its ghoulish flair, but couldn't countenance its self-parodic excesses. In February 1983 ... Palace Video released this cut version on to the video rental market, unfortunately coinciding with the rise of press-fuelled hysteria about 'video nasties'. In the panic that followed, *The Evil Dead* was cited by the Director of Public Prosecutions as potentially likely to deprave and corrupt, and a number of video dealers stocking the title were prosecuted (with varying results) under the Obscene Publications Act. In courts up and down the country, juries utterly unfamiliar with the horror genre or the audience which it attracts, were asked to respond either to key scenes from the movie or to written check-lists of the violent acts depicted therein. Unsurprisingly, their reaction tended to be one of shock – to them, the catalogue of on-screen dismemberment which the movie offered was nothing more than unashamed sadism, designed to delight those who would revel in pain. (1997, p62)

As Kermode's account continues, he makes a crucial point in any debate about the meanings of films – that audiences may watch the same film, but they *see* different films:

> Crucially this is not how the movie plays to horror fans. It's not just that the juries who considered this sadistic pleasure to be the primary function of *The Evil Dead* were over-reacting to the on-screen atrocities; it's that they were literally seeing an entirely different movie from that which had delighted *Fango* [horror comic *Fangoria*] readers the world over. To the uninitiated viewer, *The Evil Dead* was a gruelling horror picture in which human bodies were mercilessly hacked to pieces. To erudite horror fans, it was *The Three Stooges* with latex and ketchup standing in for custard pies, a knockabout romp in which everything is cranked up to eleven and in which pain and suffering play no part. (1997, p62)

Thus, the meaning of events on screen and their interpretation as 'violent' is a site of conflict and always problematic. Anecdotal evidence from the '*Evil Dead* controversy' also reveals how ludicrous was the BBFC's attempt to reduce the impact of the film through a kind of 'quantitative censorship':

> One minute of footage, including a pencil being twisted into a leg and the surviving hero being hit repeatedly over the head with an iron girder by a female zombie, was removed. 'According to Jim [Ferman],' one anonymous examiner was later to comment, 'wiggling the pencil twice was completely unacceptable, whereas wiggling it once was all right.' Stephen Woolley [of distributor Palace Pictures] also points out that the

reduction from five to three blows in the girder scene rendered the effect more horrific not less, because 'by the fifth hit on the head the audience is laughing and saying how ridiculous it all is; whereas, with the cut, the violence is sudden and much more shocking.' (Dewe Matthews, 1994, p242)

Kermode argues that

the experienced horror fan understands the on-screen action in terms of a heritage of genre knowledge which absolutely precludes the possibility of sadistic titillation. Nowhere in *The Evil Dead* does the horror fan see the actual torture, mutilation or violation of the human form (as they would do in a movie like John McNaughton's solidly unfunny *Henry: Portrait of a Serial Killer*). (1997, p63)

This notion of the competent horror viewer and the consequent renegotiation of the concept of 'violence' and its impact is reinforced by Carol Clover when she describes the interaction between audience and film in cinemas:

No one who has attended a matinee or midnight showing of a horror film with a youth audience can doubt the essentially adversarial nature of the enterprise. The performance has the quality of a cat-and-mouse game: a 'good' moment (or film) is one that 'beats' the audience, and a 'bad' moment (or film) is one in which, in effect, the audience 'wins'. Judged by plot alone, the patterns of cheering and booing seem indiscriminate or unmotivated or both. It is when they are judged by the success or failure of the film to catch the audience by surprise (or gross it out) that the patterns of cheering and booing fall into place. At such moments, the diegesis is all but short-circuited, and the horror filmmaker and the competent horror viewer come remarkably close to addressing one another directly – the viewer by shouting out his approval or disapproval not to the on-screen characters but to the people who put them there, and the people who put them there, in their turn, by marking the moment with either a tongue-in-cheek gesture ... or an actual pause to accommodate the reaction – both amounting to a silent form of second-person address. (1992, p202)

Understood in this way, the concept of cutting 'violent' chunks out of films for adult audiences starts to seem strange. **Worksheet 3** depends upon students being fairly experienced film viewers, but with the right group of learners the questions may get some worthwhile results.

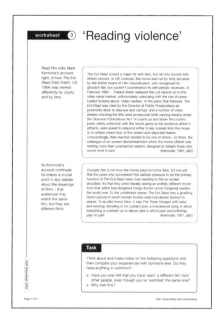

To access student worksheets and other online materials go to *Teaching Film Censorship and Controversy* at **www.bfi.org.uk/tfms** and enter User name: **filmcens@bfi.org.uk** and Password: **te1908ce**.

In the last few years, the BBFC has acknowledged the importance of context, but is still capable of sounding dogmatic in asserting what the meaning of a particular scene might be. Nevertheless, films have been passed uncut, even on video/DVD, containing scenes which, in earlier years, would have been unlikely to escape the censor's scissors. An early scene in *Irreversible* (Gaspar Noé, France, 2002), for example, in which a man is battered to death with a fire extinguisher in a sex club, survives intact because:

> The Board recognised that elements in the film may be shocking and (for many viewers) unpleasant. These, however, are not by themselves reasons for censoring them for adults. Our concern, and the public's, is principally with content which is likely to promote harmful activity. By that test, the Board was satisfied that *Irreversible* may be given a cinema release with an '18' rating. (www.bbfc.co.uk, Press Releases, 21 October 2002)

Realism is clearly a key issue here – the treatment and portrayal of violence is a major factor in how it is interpreted. Tom Dewe Matthews comments that 'In most cases the Board has ruled that unreal, stylised violence deserves more lenient treatment than the unglamorous realism of protracted death' (1994, p227) and quotes James Ferman in 1981: 'The nice thing about fantasy is all the time you can keep reminding yourself, "I can't get hurt, no one's going to get hurt, it's just make believe"' whereas 'if you present it [violence] realistically, it impinges on your feelings, you haven't got that suspension of disbelief' (1994, p228). So here we might paraphrase: fantasy violence is okay because it doesn't engage us emotionally. This would seem to be the Board's justification for granting an '18' certificate to *The Texas Chainsaw Massacre* (Tobe Hooper, USA, 1974) 24 years after initially rejecting it:

> The Board's conclusion ... was that any possible harm that might arise in terms of the effect upon a modern audience would be more than sufficiently countered by the unrealistic, even absurd, nature of the action itself. (www.bbfc.co.uk, Press Releases, 6 December 1999)

However, Ferman also commented:

> 'We are experiencing more violence now, and the danger is that by showing that as entertainment you can normalise it or legitimise it, which is something we are not prepared to do. Violence in society should always be presented as unacceptable'. (Quoted in Dewe Matthews, 1994, p228)

So here we might paraphrase: fantasy violence is a bad thing because it makes 'violence' entertaining and, by implication, violence presented more authentically might be more responsible.

This contradiction reveals the problem with any sort of definitive statement about screen violence; the construction of an event on screen as 'violent' is always dependent upon a range of contextual factors and is always, ultimately, an act of interpretation. Kevin Browne's research into the viewing habits of violent offenders (described in Barker, 2002 and Gauntlett, 2001) classifies violent films into three broad categories: 'violent drama films' (eg *Schindler's List*, Steven Spielberg, USA, 1993 and *Platoon*, Oliver Stone, USA, 1986), 'violent action films' (eg *Rambo: First Blood Part II*, George Pan Cosmatos, USA, 1985 and *Out for Justice*, John Flynn, USA, 1991) and 'violent horror films' (eg *Cannibal Holocaust*, Ruggero Deodato, USA, 1980). Despite the apparent clarity and convenience of this taxonomy, its flaws were identified by then BBFC President Andreas Whittam Smith whom, as Gauntlett tells us,

> notes that 'in practice, violent films do not always fit easily into Professor Browne's categories', since violence can be represented in more or less serious or realistic contexts. He also notes that horror films are a genre with unique conventions, and that of these films 'only a minority' fit Browne's 'violent horror' category. (2001)

Worksheet 4 is designed to produce some understanding of the codes of realism in representations of violence and to then reach some conclusions about the relationship between these and the emotional responses they generate. The examples chosen here are *Die Hard* (John McTiernan, USA, 1988) and *The Passion of the Christ* (Mel Gibson, USA, 2004). You can, of course, substitute comparable examples of your own, but these at least provide opportunities to identify the ways in which the protagonists sustain injury, the filmic codes by which this is communicated (shot type, duration, special effects) and the perception of the power relationship between protagonist and antagonist(s). One advantage of these two films is that, because students may already be familiar with the former and should know the narrative of the latter, it is possible to provide contextual information quickly before showing clips. Select clips according to what's appropriate for you and your students; the flaying scenes in *The Passion of the Christ* are gruelling, so the earlier arrest and beating scenes may be more appropriate for classroom screening and discussion.

> To access student worksheets and other online materials go to *Teaching Film Censorship and Controversy* at **www.bfi.org.uk/tfms** and enter User name: **filmcens@bfi.org.uk** and Password: **te1908ce**.

worksheet ④ Violence and realism

Watch *Die Hard* (John McTiernan, USA, 1988) and *The Passion of the Christ* (Mel Gibson, USA, 2004), or relevant extracts.

● Compare a scene from each in which violence is done to the protagonist.
  – Are there any similarities?
  – Are there any differences?
  – Break down the ways in which the violence acts are represented in the table below:

	Die Hard	The Passion of the Christ
Action		
Duration		
Shot type(s)		
Sound		
Special effects		
Consequences for victim		
Does it feel 'real'? Why?		
Is it upsetting or distressing?		

The 'effects' model

Violence and sexual violence are such major issues for the Board because of a deeply (culturally) embedded notion that films may be 'harmful' to some audiences and/or to society in general. Despite the absence of any conclusive research we often find a 'cause and effect' model of the relationship between text and audience is cited as a justification for age certification, cutting and, in the case of the press (see below), calls for even greater censorship. So, the distributor of *Lara Croft: Tomb Raider* (Simon West, USA/Germany/UK/Japan, 2001) accepted the Board's insistence on cuts in order to get a '12' certificate on the grounds that it included glamorisation of weapons (which might, presumably, encourage children to use them) and imitable techniques:

> The natural audience for *Lara Croft* is the 12 to 15 age group, but the Board's Classification Guidelines make it clear that at '12' the glamorisation of weapons such as knives and the graphic illustration of dangerous techniques such as head-butts and throat chops are unacceptable. (www.bbfc.co.uk, Press Releases, 29 June 2001)

Similarly, although at a different age classification, the video of *The Driller Killer* (Abel Ferrara, USA, 1979) 'pre-cut by the distributor to remove the more extreme and unacceptable images' has been rendered 'unlikely to produce any harmful effects, either upon its audience or on society more generally' (www.bbfc.co.uk, Press Releases, 2 June 1999).

This notion of 'harm' prevails in discussions about censorship and, while most informed opinion has moved away from the *direct* 'cause and effect' model (for adult viewing at least), the emphasis has shifted to a concern about wider social effects that may result from audiences consuming 'violent' media products. We can identify this in James Ferman's comment that:

> I totally reject the cause and effect argument, I don't think any film that I can remember has had a direct effect and caused a crime, except possibly, and it's twenty years since I saw it ... *A Clockwork Orange*, where there were attacks on tramps afterwards and there were some rapes that appeared to be inspired by that film ... I've never checked up those stories and they may not be true at all, but I think it's much more the 'drip drip' effect. (*The Last Days of the Board*, 1999)

We find a similar criticism from Kim Howells (then Culture Minister) in 2003 arguing that 'the constant diet of death and destruction in modern film and television has created a "pornography of violence", appealing to viewers' lowest urges.' (Akwagyiram, 2003). Similarly, the BBFC's refusal to grant a video certificate to *Banned from Television*, 'a compilation of scenes of extremely violent death, injury and mutilation' which 'invites enjoyment at human suffering' is explained thus:

> The Board has concluded that the video is potentially harmful because of the influence it may have on the attitudes and behaviour of a significant proportion of likely viewers. The instinct of concern and compassion for the suffering of others is a basic social necessity. So is respect for the dignity of real human life. By presenting actual human death and mutilation as entertainment, the work, in the Board's view has the potential to erode these instincts. There is a danger of it falling into the hands of young and impressionable persons (whatever its classification) and of some significant brutalising effect on their attitude to human life and pain. (www.bbfc.co.uk, Press Releases, 2 June 1999)

This interpretation of the possible effects of media texts is inevitably speculative, as a senior BBFC examiner freely admits,

> The Board looks at the whole range of research and takes the view that no one researcher (and certainly no one piece of research) can be considered able to reveal the definitive truth about media effects. In such a disputed area, any individual piece of research must be considered in the light of the full body of evidence, a body which is often as contradictory as it is disputed. (P Johnson, email, 19 May 2004)

It is the nature of some of this research that is often problematic. David Gauntlett (2001), with reference to Kevin Browne's 1998 research, 'Effects of Video

Violence on Young Offenders', draws our attention to the fact that the report's summary clearly states 'The research cannot prove whether video violence causes crime' and describes the study as 'refreshingly different, in that it took offenders rather than screen violence as its starting point'. However 'it still went awry because the researchers imposed a media-centred approach onto the data', in other words, because the researchers succumbed to the seductions of the 'effects model', the notion that a certain kind of quantifiable input results in a certain kind of measurable output. Gauntlett (2001) goes on to describe 'Ten things wrong with the effects model'. His points are summarised below:

1. The effects model tackles social problems 'backwards'
To understand the causes of violence, or other human behaviour, research should logically begin with the people who engage in those actions. Media effects researchers, however, begin with the idea that the media is to blame, and then try to make links from the product back to the world of actual violence.

2. The effects model treats children as inadequate
Much of the discourse about children and the media positions children as potential victims, and as little else. Furthermore, media effects research usually employs methods which will not allow children to challenge this assumption. The hundreds of shallow quantitative studies, often conducted by 'psychologists', have often been little more than traps for their subjects.

3. Assumptions within the effects model are characterised by barely concealed conservative ideology
Media effects research is good news for conservatives and right-wing 'moralists'. Conservatives have traditionally liked to blame popular culture for the ailments of society, not only because they fear new and innovative forms of media, but also because it allows them to divert attention away from other and, for them, more awkward social questions such as levels of welfare provision.

4. The effects model inadequately defines its own objects of study
Media effects studies are usually extremely undiscriminating about how they identify worrying bits of media content, or subsequent behaviour by viewers. An act of 'violence', for example, might be smashing cages to set animals free or using force to disable a nuclear-armed plane. In many studies, 'verbal aggression' is included as a form of aggression. Once processed by effects research, all of these various depictions or actions simply emerge as a 'level of aggression'.

5. The effects model is often based on artificial studies
Since careful sociological studies of media influences require considerable amounts of time and money, they are heavily outnumbered by simpler studies which often put their subjects into artificial and contrived situations (but are then presented as if they are studies of the everyday world). In these settings the

behaviour of children towards an inanimate object is often taken to represent how they would behave towards a real person.

6. The effects model is often based on studies with misapplied methodology

Studies which do not rely on the experimental method (such as longitudinal studies, in which a group is assessed over a period of time) often fall down by wrongly applying methodological procedure or by drawing inappropriate conclusions from particular methods. This means, for example, applying different measures of TV viewing and levels of aggressiveness at different times, or ignoring the importance of biological, developmental and environmental factors. Correlation studies may leap to dubious causal conclusions: there is a logical coherence to the idea that children whose behaviour is antisocial and disruptive will also have a greater interest in the more violent and noisy television programmes, whereas the idea that their behaviour is a *consequence* of these programmes lacks both rational consistency and empirical support.

7. The effects model is selective in its criticisms of media depictions of violence

Effects studies may involve distinctly ideological interpretations of what constitutes 'antisocial' action and tend only to refer to fictional TV programmes and films rather than news and factual programming. There is a substantial problem with an approach which suggests that on-screen violence is bad if it does not extend this to cover news and factual violence, which is often cruel and has no visible consequences for the perpetrator.

8. The effects model assumes researchers' superiority to the 'masses'

While the researchers consider that other people might be affected by media content, they assume that their own approach is objective and that the media will have no effect on them. Surveys show that almost everybody feels this way: while varying percentages of the population say they are concerned about media effects on others, almost nobody says they have been affected themselves. Some researchers excuse this approach by saying that their concerns lie with children. However, in cases where this is not possible, because young adults have been used in the study, we find the researchers' invocation of the 'Other', the undiscriminating 'heavy viewer', the 'uneducated', or the working class as the victim of 'effects'.

9. The effects model makes no attempt to understand the meanings of the media

The effects model rests on a base of reductive assumptions about and unjustified stereotypes of media content. To assert that 'media violence' will bring about negative consequences is not only to presume that depictions of violence in the media always promote antisocial behaviour, and that such a category actually exists and makes sense, but it also assumes that whatever medium is being studied by the researchers holds a singular message which will be carried unproblematically to the audience. In-depth qualitative studies have given strong support to the view that media audiences routinely arrive at their own, often diverse, interpretations of everyday media texts.

10. The effects model is not grounded in theory

How does seeing an action depicted by the media actually prompt an individual to behave in the same way? The lack of convincing explanations (let alone anything we could call a theory) of how this process might occur is perhaps the most important and worrying problem with effects research. There is the idea that violence is 'glamorised' in some films and TV shows, which sometimes seems relevant; however, the more horrifyingly violent a production is, the less the violence tends to be glamorised. Even in the case of *The Matrix* (Andy Wachowski/Larry Wachowski, USA/Australia, 1999), in which serious violence looks rather stylish, there is no good explanation of why anyone would simply copy those actions; and we do need an explanation if the effects hypothesis is to rise above the status of a 'not very convincing suggestion'.

These notes are reproduced as notes for students, available at www.bfi.org.uk/tfms. (Enter User name: **filmcens@bfi.org.uk** and Password: **te1908ce**.)

This last example is a useful one given the desperate (and unsuccessful) attempts of American defence lawyers to invoke 'The Matrix Defence'. The lawyers of one of the Washington snipers, Lee Boyd Malvot, claimed he was insane and indoctrinated with 'Matrix-like philosophies'. In 2003 in Fairfax, Virginia, Rachel Fierro, the defence attorney for Joshua Cooke, on trial for killing his parents, tried to get her client a psychiatric evaluation by citing *The Matrix* as a factor. The evidence she produced to support this claim was far from convincing:

> The evidence that he was obsessed with the movie *The Matrix* was all of the props that he had: the poster, the long black trench coat, the movie; the fact that he watched it so often; the way he acted out the actual murders, having the twelve gauge pump action shotgun similar to that used by the main character. All of those things evolved as characteristics of the movie *The Matrix*.

And in an interview on CNN, faced with the pertinent question 'millions of people have seen this movie and ... haven't actually killed anyone, millions have seen it, so how can you use it as a defence?', she weakly replies: 'Well it was clear after an investigation of the facts of this case and after a careful review of the evidence that Joshua Cooke was obsessed with the movie *The Matrix*' (The Matrix *Defence*, Channel 4, 2003).

Although 'laboratory experiments' may now be falling out of fashion in relation to films and videos, this methodology is still considered to have some usefulness regarding video games. A Channel 4 *Dispatches* programme from 2000 provides vivid evidence of some of David Gauntlett's concerns about research in the effects tradition. The programme's rhetoric and tropes will be examined below, but the demonstrations of research can provide students with some valuable examples of how a specific agenda passes itself off as neutral and 'scientific'.

Presenter Joe Layburn introduces the research with the very reasonable

> Clearly not every child who plays violent video games becomes violent, but that doesn't mean parents can relax. What's your child like when he's been blasting zombies or fighting ninjas? Notice any changes? It could be that a whole generation of children is at risk from the more subtle effects of violent video games.

He then goes on to establish the credentials of the work: 'Our experiment has been designed for us by the Psychology Department at the University of East London. It will be published as a scientific paper later this year.' Professor Brian Clifford, in charge of the research states that 'The purpose of this study was to see if in some way the thought patterns of children were changed as a result of playing a violent and a non-violent game.'

We then see children playing video games in 'laboratory conditions' and are told that one group played a 'non-violent' video game. The other 50 played 'the beat 'em up *Shaolin* (martial arts game rated suitable for 11-year-olds and over)'. The follow-up entails each boy being questioned independently about a set of images:

> After playing for just 10 minutes both groups were asked to look at a set of ambiguous photos. One photo shows a group of boys in a school playground – one is picking up a ball, looking at the camera. Test subjects are asked, 'the ball's just hit you on the back of the head – was it deliberate?' Boys who played the non-violent game tended to see it as an accident, but what about the boys who played the violent game?

We witness the following exchange (which, incidentally, takes place in a darkened room with a video camera pointing at the subject):

> Researcher: Why did the ball hit you in the head?
> Boy: Because he's kicked it at me.
> Researcher: So do you think he did it on purpose or by accident?
> Boy: On purpose.
> Researcher: Okay. What would you do after the ball hit you in the head?
> Boy: I'd be annoyed and probably shout at him.
> Researcher: Okay. How do you think this boy feels? What's he thinking after the ball hit you?
> Boy: I think he's a bit worried that I might hit him, but inside I think he's kind of laughing at me.
> Researcher: He's laughing at you?
> Boy: Yeah.

You can get a copy of this programme from www.richmond-utcoll.ac.uk/facilities/video.asp

The conclusions of this experiment are summarised by Professor Brian Clifford:

> 'Consistently the children who played the violent video game interpreted these ambiguous stimuli, these ambiguous photographs, in a more hostile way than did the children who played the non-violent game.'

The presenter, to ensure that the point is clear, says 'so time and again, when you tested them, they saw the world as a mean place rather than a good place if they'd just finished playing the violent game.' In a voiceover he reiterates:

> 'Our experiment suggests that violent video games make even good kids view the world as more hostile. They're more likely to talk about punishing those who've upset them. But talking is one thing – could a video game make you hurt someone in real life?'

The programme implicitly 'proves' this when it moves on to some more laboratory testing of the measurable negative effects of video games:

> Dr Mary Ballard [Appalachian State University] did her research on 120 college students which allowed her to test some of the more violent games on the market. She's going to recreate for us her most significant study so far. The game – *Mortal Kombat*, a martial arts slug-fest where, among other things, you can rip out your opponent's spine. The players – gentle giant Bobby on the left, and me. After 15 minutes' fighting Dr Ballard tells Bobby he's going to give me a memory test of word pairs I'm supposed to have learned – it's actually a ruse to see how aggressive he's become. When I get a right answer Bobby's to reward me with some jellybeans, if I get it wrong he gets to punish me. To punish me Bobby plunges my hand into a tank of ice-cold water – how long he decides to keep it there will show how aggressive he's become. [Sinister synthesised music plays in background as we watch 'gentle giant' Bobby holding Joe's hand in the ice tank when Joe gets a question wrong.] What's crucial is that the 30 people in the original experiment who played a non-violent video game did not show aggression like this. (*Dispatches*, Channel 4, 2000)

Worksheet 5 invites students to challenge the assumptions and execution of effects research with specific reference to the examples in this programme. Even without reference to Gauntlett's 'Ten things wrong with the effects model' list, students will see some gaping holes in the conclusions drawn and some serious questions to be asked about the methods used. For example, in relation to the first experiment, students might ask:

- Is the boys' imaginative interpretation of the photographs the same as having a hostile world view?
- Can the fantasy game playing of *Shaolin* be unproblematically described as 'violent'?
- Can the setting and structure of the interviews determine the boys' responses?
- What does 'consistently' mean in statistical terms?

- Which criteria are used to define a response as 'hostile'?
- Even if it were possible to prove a tendency towards a hostile world view, wouldn't it be necessary to demonstrate the ways in which this putative hostility was translated into action?
- How long after playing the game would the violent action need to be performed in order to prove that it had been caused by putative hostility?

1 of 2 pages

To access student worksheets and other online materials go to *Teaching Film Censorship and Controversy* at **www.bfi.org.uk/tfms** and enter User name: **filmcens@bfi.org.uk** and Password: **te1908ce**.

Many of the same questions can be asked about Mary Ballard's research:

- Can the game simply be called 'violent'?
- What was the 'non-violent' game played by other participants?
- How might the setting for the experiment influence the responses?
- Is plunging someone's hand into icy water in a laboratory the same as being violent in the real world?
- How many other variables might be at work here – can we be sure that Bobby really is a 'gentle giant'?
- In order to contrast like with like wouldn't it be necessary to test the same 30 people with a 'non-violent' and 'violent' game?

The conclusion overall will probably be that these researchers have a pre-existing idea of what they would like to find and that they use crude instruments and far from neutral procedures in order to 'reveal' this.

Alternatives to the 'effects model'

An alternative to focusing on texts and attempting to determine their meaning by subjecting them to more or less scientific processes is to attempt to understand the meanings produced by audiences. David Buckingham (1993), Martin Barker (Barker et al, 2001) and Annette Hill (1997) have all directed their attention to the ways in which audiences view films and television, the knowledge they bring to them, their expectations and, crucially, their viewing competence. The political impact of this kind of work is that it makes it difficult to sustain paternalistic arguments which legitimise acts of censorship and cutting; rather than seeing the audience as infantile and in need of protection, it demonstrates the ability of audiences to make active decisions to view 'violent' material, to make sense of it in a variety of ways and, in some cases, to censor their own viewing.

In *Shocking Entertainment*, Hill suggests that

> There are more productive ways to debate screen violence. By productive, I mean that there are areas of investigation other than the cause-effect debate, which will prove useful to those interested in the process of viewing violence.

She argues that

> Active consumers of violent movies possess 'portfolios of interpretation'. This means that viewers utilize a number of reactive mechanisms in order to interpret fictional violence. These methods include:
>
> ● Anticipating violent images/scenes;
> ● Building character relationships;
> ● Self-censoring fictional violence;
> ● Testing boundaries.
>
> ... By developing 'portfolios of interpretation', consumers of violent movies demonstrate how complex and dynamic the process of viewing violence can be. (1997, pp4–5)

Hill's aim in this study is '... not to reach statistical conclusions about who watches violent movies but to test and to develop my own hypotheses regarding the process of viewing violence' (p9). It is worth summarising Hill's methods in order to provide a research model for students which contrasts with the more obvious effects-led approaches already outlined.

Choosing the films: In order to include films which are 'violent', Hill uses 'societal/cultural consensus' to identify eight candidates – *Reservoir Dogs* (Quentin Tarantino, USA, 1992), *Pulp Fiction* (Quentin Tarantino, USA, 1994), *True Romance* (Tony Scott, USA, 1993), *Natural Born Killers* (Oliver Stone, USA, 1994), *Man Bites Dog* (Remy Belvaux/André Bonzel/Benoit Poelvoorde, Belgium, 1992), *Henry: Portrait of a Serial Killer* (John McNaughton, USA, 1986),

Bad Lieutenant (Abel Ferrara, USA, 1992) and *Killing Zoe* (Roger Avary, France/USA, 1994). She refers to a range of press reports which seem to identify these as a 'new wave' of violent movies, as well as textual factors:

> What these movies share, in terms of content, is a preoccupation with violence towards the individual, as opposed to the state, and, in terms of style, the use of realism when representing violence. (p11)

Choosing research methods: Individual interviews and questionnaires were piloted but found unsatisfactory. The questionnaire was inadequate for the task of gaining insight into the complex response to viewing violence and the interviews 'lacked an interaction of ideas … necessary to understanding the process of viewing violence, an activity which is more social than individual' (p8). Consequently focus groups were chosen because 'they provide an opportunity to collect data from group interaction.'

Choosing participants: The criteria used were:
- Participants must be over 18 years old.
- Participants must have seen three or more films on the target list.
- Participants must not be engaged in any research in this field.

This was to ensure that Hill recruited 'current consumers of violent movies who did not have a clear agenda, but who did have an active interest in the research subject'. A gender balance was sought, but otherwise the research did not constitute a representative survey in terms of class and ethnicity. Participants were recruited initially through posters or direct address outside cinemas and then by follow-up phone calls and letters explaining the nature of the focused discussions.

Conducting the focus groups: A pilot group enabled Hill to test the questions. Subsequently the focus group discussions, with groups of four to six, took place on Saturday afternoons in a hired restaurant with wine and refreshments. The rationale for this was to provide a neutral, safe environment. Discussions, lasting two and quarter hours, involved showing stimulus material (clips from the chosen films), then inviting responses, attempting to create the conditions for relaxed interaction. As moderator, Hill posed the same questions in each group in order to ensure reliability and validity and, with an assistant moderator and audio-recording equipment, had three 'data collection points' in order to ensure accuracy. Questions were divided into opening questions ('How do you choose to see these movies?'), transition questions ('Going to the cinema is a social activity – do you notice how other people respond to violent scenes in a film?') and key questions ('Do you identify with any one character in this scene?').

Hill's summary of her research, while tentative and acknowledging its dependence upon a relatively small sample, highlights findings such as:

- Violent movies test viewers and consumers are aware of this.

- Viewing violence is a social activity.
- Anticipation is a key factor in determining response to violence.
- Consumer choice influences character relationships.
- Thresholds reaffirm social taboos and individual experience.
- Viewers use a variety of methods to self-censor violence.
- Boundary testing is part of the process of viewing violence.
- Real violence is raw and brutal and not entertaining.
- Fictional violence is entertaining.
- The safety of violent movies.

For students, Hill's work provides a model of audience-centred research – an alternative approach to the 'scientific' text-centred approach. **Worksheet 6** provides students with an opportunity to devise their own research into the relationship between media and audiences.

To access student worksheets and other online materials go to *Teaching Film Censorship and Controversy* at **www.bfi.org.uk/tfms** and enter User name: **filmcens@bfi.org.uk** and Password: **te1908ce**.

They may decide, of course, that they wish to conduct a 'scientific' experiment, but will have to justify this approach when they answer the questions about method and rationale.

● Corrupting the young

Fears about harming young people, or worse, transforming young people into monsters, seem to have always been high on the list of priorities for censors and moral campaigners. Richard Falcon explains that even at the beginning of the 20th century, local authorities routinely refused certificates to films due to concerns about their effects on young people (1994, p12). One of the things at stake here is a particular conception of childhood, or rather, a range of concepts of childhood, often contradictory, sometimes mutually exclusive. As described above, a great deal of research is charged with the business of identifying the negative influence of the media on children. Below there are examples of how different elements of the media mobilise different versions of childhood in order to persuade us that 'our' angelic children are in danger of being damaged, or that 'other' devilish children have already metamorphosed into something uncontrollable because of the ill effects of the media.

The Video Recordings Act 1984 includes a clause requiring that classification must have 'special regard to the likelihood of video works being viewed in the family home', which, as Dewe Matthews says '... could be taken to mean that any video image which could upset a child old enough to recognise what was on the television screen should be banned' (1994, p246). A useful exercise with students is to tease out some of these assumptions about the nature of childhood and their possible susceptibility to ill effects. **Worksheet 7** asks for a personal response to film in relation to a notional younger audience. An alternative is to play a representative extract from a '12'- or '15'- rated video (for example, *Lara Croft: Tomb Raider* (Simon West, USA/Germany/UK/Japan, 2001), or *Spider-Man* (Sam Raimi, USA, 2002)) to elicit similar responses.

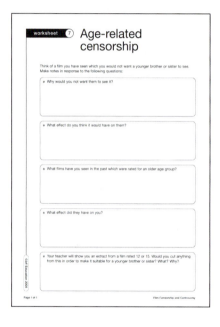

To access student worksheets and other online materials go to *Teaching Film Censorship and Controversy* at **www.bfi.org.uk/tfms** and enter User name: **filmcens@bfi.org.uk** and Password: **te1908ce**.

● Controversy and the press

Controversy around films and videos is often fuelled by newspapers and television programmes, and it's worth examining some examples in order to identify how specific fears are mobilised and how particular tropes are used. The *Dispatches* programme previously discussed, for example, combines a sensational mode of address with the gravity of science:

For the first time on television we test the psychological effects of the new wave of violent video games. 100 British school kids have helped us, along with leading scientists. And we look at remarkable new research from America on how video games can change your behaviour – you'll be shocked by the results.

In addition, the programme draws upon the alarming notion of 'immersion' in order to persuade us that this 'new' technology constitutes a new threat:

So what are these games and who's playing them? There are 'beat 'em ups', 'smash 'em ups', 'shoot 'em ups', and, unlike violent films that you just sit and watch, you're in the thick of the action. Take *Quake 3* where you point the weapon, you pull the trigger, you get rewarded for killing.

Predictably, we find an appeal to notional parents to protect their children from the products of profit-driven corporations: 'The makers say the really violent games aren't meant for children ... in the real world children are getting their hands on violent video games.'

And, backed up with the rhetoric of the image and the spurious information that an amusement arcade is in the vicinity of a school where a shooting occurred: 'Today at the arcade close to the school, kids as young as seven play shooting games with staggering skill.' The camera zooms in to an ECU (extreme close-up) of a child's eyes as he plays a video game.

We also find a vocabulary which mobilises images of sickness, 'unnaturalness' and antisocial behaviour:

A video arcade in Jonesborough, Arkansas. This was a regular haunt of two young killers who went on a shooting spree at their school two years ago. Both boys were avid players of violent video games.

Inevitably we also find the testimony of an expert. Lieutenant Colonel Dave Grossman (introduced as 'a military psychologist – expert in how soldiers learn to kill') tells us:

In the violent video games I blow Billy's stinking head off countless thousands of times, and do I get in trouble? No I get points – do you understand? We've taken healthy play and we've turned it on its head and we reward you for the very thing that you should have been punished for. And we nurture behaviour in children at very young ages that is pathological. (*Dispatches*, Channel 4, 2000)

Journalism routinely invokes metaphors of disaster and assault when discussing the relationship between media and audience, such as this headline and standfirst from the *Observer Magazine*:

Cruising for a bruising: Flick on the telly and you're bombarded with violent images from Baghdad to Brookside. But do they do any lasting harm? Clint Witchalls goes 10 rounds with the remote. (Witchalls, 2004)

One's eye is then drawn to the central image from the documentary-style fiction film *Man Bites Dog*, in which the main character points a gun (hugely magnified through wide-angle distortion) off screen. The picture is captioned: 'Gunning for it: new evidence shows that watching violence changes the way our brains perform.' The writer describes watching television on a Sunday night and describes what he sees in terms of bodily violations (a car bombing on the news, a documentary about facelifts) and tells us

> I've just seen two horrific events, which, given the clarity of the digital images, could just as well have taken place in my living room, yet I'm unmoved. But am I unaffected? Is this blitzkrieg of violent images doing something to my psyche?

The article is actually a review of a new book about how forms of post-traumatic stress disorder might result from 'violent images on TV' (including those of 9/11, but not differentiating this from fictional forms of 'violence'). However, the combination of visual and verbal rhetoric, pseudo-science and general vagueness about distinctions between real violence and screen violence, and between different sorts of on-screen depictions of violence, all lead to a persuasively scary conclusion:

> Thus it would appear wise for many of us to avoid exposing ourselves to traumatic events, including those depicted in the media, that might increase our long-term vulnerability to trauma.

Other examples of journalistic hyperbole might include metaphors of addiction and obsession, as well as the sort of threats of attack or immersion, invocations of science ('new evidence', a 'new report') and appeals to a universal community of parenthood. Sometimes this can culminate in a call to arms, exemplified after the killing of James Bulger when *The Sun* cried out: 'For the sake of all our kids burn your video nasty.' This is an important aspect of the censorship and controversy area. As Martin Barker (1984, 1997) has shown, the press perform a significant role in mobilising 'common sense' against film and video violence. Specific examples should be analysed in terms of their use of rhetoric and the qualities of their argument, which can lead to a creative writing exercise (**Worksheet 8**) intended to provide an opportunity to 'knowingly' put these journalistic techniques into practice. Another version of this exercise is to provide a piece of stimulus material, such as the *Child's Play 3* video cover, and ask students what they know of the case associated with it. They can then attempt to write an appropriate tabloid article that might have been produced at the time. This process of ascertaining the power of the news media to offer a particular definitive, long-lasting version of events has been used by the Glasgow Media Group in relation to the coal dispute of the 1980s; it was found that students shown an image of picketing miners reproduced the dominant version of events (sometimes replicating key phrases exactly) as offered by TV news at the time.

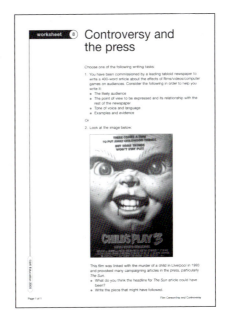

● Sex and nudity

There has been a significant shift in the last few years towards a much greater degree of liberalism concerning the depiction of (consensual) sexual activity on screen. The BBFC guidelines suggest that while the Board

> respects the right of adults to choose their own entertainment, within the law [and] will therefore expect to intervene only rarely in relation to '18' rated cinema films … [it] may, however, cut or reject … the more explicit images of sexual activity – unless they can be exceptionally justified by context.

In addition, 'material which appears to be simulated is generally passed '18', while images of real sex are confined to the "R18" category.'

Despite this last statement, there are now several examples of unsimulated sex at '18' and, although it is unlikely that anyone would want to watch these with students, it is necessary to become familiar with the debates and issues around such depictions of sexual activity.

Before looking at some of these debates, it is worth identifying the enormous difference between the Board's attitude to nudity today and its attitude in the past. The current guidelines state that 'natural nudity, providing there is no sexual context or sub-text, is acceptable at all classification levels', which means that this is possible even at certificate 'U'. At '12A' (and '12' on video) 'nudity is allowed, but in a sexual context will be brief and discreet' and 'sexual activity may be implied', and at '15' 'sexual activity and nudity may be portrayed but without strong detail'. This is a far cry from 1958 when under John Trevelyan, Secretary of the BBFC,

> ... breasts and buttocks, but not genitalia, would be accepted by the Board 'provided that the setting was recognisable as a nudist camp or nature reserve'. (Dewe Matthews, 1994, p169)

By 1968 the Board was able to pass a full frontal nude shot in *If...* (Lindsay Anderson, UK, 1968) of Mrs Kemp, the housemaster's wife, walking naked down a corridor, perhaps because the director appealed to John Trevelyan as one who could appreciate a work of artistic merit:

> Mrs Kemp, he wrote to Trevelyan, 'in the dormitory corridor, I am hoping will be so obviously aesthetic as to avoid any suggestion of offence. It reveals no more, after all, than any member of the public can see at the National Gallery free of charge.' (Dewe Matthews, 1994, p177)

There was more resistance to male nudity, even in works with 'artistic merit', as the discussions about *Women in Love* (Ken Russell, UK, 1969) reveal. The problem scene – in which Oliver Reed and Alan Bates wrestle naked – led to Trevelyan asking Russell to remove the full-length shots in which their genitals were clearly visible. Even after Russell removed these shots and darkened others there was still anxiety about these 'extreme scenes', but with an understanding that the 'quality and integrity of the film' justified them (Dewe Matthews, 1994, p180).

There are a couple of things worth examining more closely here; firstly the notion of nudity as a taboo (and therefore, something with the power to shock) and secondly the notion of 'artistic merit' as a justification for stretching or breaking existing boundaries. Despite their power to shock at the time, *Women in Love* and *If...* are not controversial today and students could use them as examples in a historical narrative about representations of naked bodies becoming acceptable on screen – what has been the nature of the cultural investment in keeping bodies clothed and how has this evolved? They could also address the issue of why there has been greater resistance to naked male bodies on screen than female bodies – Dewe Matthews suggests that

> For the film censors ... male genitalia are the most taboo-ridden area of human anatomy. Probably this is because of the masculine monopoly of the BBFC – not to mention the establishment at large – and the notorious heterosexual male aversion to the exposure and resultant demystification of the male crotch. (1994, p178)

The second point – the notion of 'artistic merit' – is one that obtains today as a justification for including explicit representations of sexual activity. *Baise-moi* (Virginie Despentes/Coralie Trinh Thi, France, 2000) includes a number of scenes of unsimulated sex and is described by the BBFC as a serious and well-made film. It concerns the reaction of two young women to the violence and humiliation habitually visited upon them by men. It represents an important viewpoint. The explicit images illustrate the theme which is bleak and, for many viewers, profoundly unpleasant. It would be less effectively rendered if cuts were made to the later scenes to reduce its angry frankness. (www.bbfc.co.uk, Press Releases, 26 February 2001)

Similarly, regarding *Romance* (Catherine Breillat, France, 1999), which the BBFC passed at '18' without cuts, the justification given is that

> ... the film offers insights about the female condition, about the difficulty of separating sex from love and about the ties of fidelity. No doubt there will be a range of opinion as to its depth and quality. With its overlay of philosophical commentary, it is a particularly French piece. It is also very French in the frank way it addresses sexual issues. The BBFC is in no doubt that *Romance* is a serious work. It contains, however, a few scenes which include quite explicitly sexual imagery. The Board's relevant test of acceptability for '18' certification is set out in its published Guidelines: 'Images of real sex will usually be brief and must be justified by context.' In *Romance*, the most explicit portrayal of sexual intercourse is avoided. But there are occasional strong images of male genitalia of which the strongest is set within a 'safe sex' context. (www.bbfc.co.uk, Press Releases, 29 July 1999)

The most recent example of the BBFC's increasing liberalisation regarding representations of sex is its response to Michael Winterbottom's *9 Songs* (UK, 2004), a film tracing the arc of a relationship and described as 'a non-pornographic film with two actors playing lovers and having real sex on film' (Jeffries, 2005). Derek Malcolm (2004) describes the film as

> easily the most sexually explicit to be made by a mainstream British director [which] is likely to be considered hard core rather than porn. The difference between the two may be largely a matter of semantics. But it could be argued that porn is for voyeurs and simply about sex, whereas 'hard core' could sometimes be about love as well as physical grappling.

Despite the fact that Anne Widdecombe failed to make this distinction, arguing that 'It is not the Board's role to allow pornography to enter the mainstream' (Hastings, 2004), the BBFC classified *9 Songs* '18' for cinema release, explaining its decision in this way:

> Some people may find such explicit images shocking or unexpected in a cinema film. The Board is sensitive to public concerns, and its Guidelines are based on extensive consultation. The Board's Guidelines allow the more explicit images of sexual activity at '18' if they can be exceptionally justified by context. The Board has concluded in this case that adults should be free to choose whether or not to see the film. The film does not raise issues of harm or sexual violence. The film's exploration of the relationship provides sufficient contextual justification for the Board to

pass the work uncut at '18'. *9 Songs* is wholly different in appearance, tone, intention and treatment from the sex works which the Board classifies either at '18' or 'R18' (and which in the latter case may be supplied only in licensed sex shops). (www.bbfc.co.uk, Press Releases, 18 October 2004)

The key words here are 'appearance, tone, intention and treatment', in which regard Winterbottom's film has managed to satisfy the BBFC that it is not primarily intended to arouse, but that it is finding a new way to tell its story. The film was subsequently submitted for video/DVD release and again passed without cuts, so the Board clearly decided that, in this case, the requirement of the Video Recordings Act (to have special regard to the likelihood of video works being viewed in the home) did not constitute a problem. A distinction is being made, therefore, between the style, tone and intention of 'sex works' (pornography) which the BBFC passes at 'R18', making them only available through licensed sex shops, and films such as *9 Songs* where, despite the inclusion of unsimulated sex, the style, tone and intention are perceived to be different.

A theoretical question you may wish to explore in relation to such examples is that of representation. In most films with sex scenes, we have on screen a representation of two performers pretending to have sex; in *9 Songs*, *Romance* and *Baise-moi* we have a representation of two performers actually having sex, albeit 'still performing sex rather than doing what lovers do when they are not being filmed for an audience of strangers' (Jeffries, 2005). What effect might this shift in the 'signified' have on our suspension of disbelief? Arguably it might enhance the realism, but equally the case might be made that this irruption of reality into a fiction might destabilise our investment in the *fictional* relationship.

● Sexual violence

This is potentially an uncomfortable area to explore with students, but as sexual violence is perhaps the BBFC's primary concern, it is important to understand the issues and have some examples which illustrate the implementation of this concern. Most of the BBFC's 'problem films' have been problematic because of a perception of sexualised violence against women, an approach that seems to have been consolidated under James Ferman, who apparently told one of his female examiners that 'You don't understand, I'm a better feminist than women are' (Dewe Matthews, 1994, p223).

It is not necessary for students to view these problem films in order to understand the issues (**Worksheet 9** provides a 'paper-based' opportunity to get to grips with the issues); indeed it would be a miserable experience to analyse rape scenes in detail to ascertain whether their treatment constituted 'titillation' or a brutally realistic 'anti-rape' message. But making a distinction between the two is the key issue and, as always, coming to a conclusion depends upon treatment and interpretation. Kermode (2001) describes the conflict between the BBFC and Blue Underground, the distributors of Wes Craven's *The Last House on the Left* (USA, 1972), as one of differing interpretations:

> [Robin] Duval [then Director of the BBFC] wrote to Blue Underground restating his commitment to outlawing the film on the grounds that it contained 'gross violence committed against women, often in a context with clear sexual overtones. It invites the viewer to relish the detail of the violence and killings.' Blue Underground sees the film in an entirely different way: 'The BBFC's interpretation of *The Last House on the Left* as "erotic" would appear to be quite unique. Reviewers over the years have invariably referred to the cold, flat, dispassionate style of the film-making – quite the opposite of "erotica" in fact.'

To access student worksheets and other online materials go to *Teaching Film Censorship and Controversy* at **www.bfi.org.uk/tfms** and enter User name: **filmcens@bfi.org.uk** and Password: **te1908ce**.

A more recent controversial film, Gaspar Noé's *Irreversible*, has attracted similarly divergent interpretations of its central rape scene. The BBFC, which passed the film '18' uncut for cinema and on video, states:

> Depictions which eroticise or appear to endorse sexual violence are of particular concern both to the BBFC and to the public. With this in mind, the Board took advice from a clinical forensic psychiatrist about the rape scene in particular. She agreed with the Board that the scene is a harrowing and vivid portrayal of the brutality of rape. However, it contains no explicit sexual images and is not designed to titillate. The Board was satisfied, therefore, that no issue of harm arose in the context of a cinema release for adult viewing only ... If [the film] is submitted for video

release the Board will need to consider any potential for harm that might arise from the rape scene being taken out of context and viewed repeatedly. (www.bbfc.co.uk, Press Releases, 21 October 2002)

Leslie Felperin, however, asserts that

> The film's S&M tactics and moral murkiness are most pronounced in the rape sequence. The fulcrum of the movie, the scene is all about provocation, from the shimmering flesh-coloured satin dress that seems painted on Monica Bellucci's perfect body (caressingly shot for maximum effect when violated), to the angle from which we watch the rape take place. Some have argued that because the camera sits unflinchingly throughout the nine-minute rape, and remains a few feet away during the beating, the scene is not exploitative, as if coolly discreet *mise en scène* automatically annuls identification with the rapist. Similarly it's been argued that the very duration of the sequence drives home the atrocity of the act of rape. (2003, p48)

It seems likely that if the BBFC or one of its advisors had identified what Felperin noticed, its response would have been different. The example highlights the difficulty of interpretation and the need to take into account a range of textual factors, such as shot type, duration, sound and *mise en scène* – Nick James, for example, refers to 'the glamorously sexualised Alex (Monica Bellucci) wearing a flimsy one-piece string-tied dress that emphasises her nipples' (James and Kermode, 2003, p21).

I Spit on Your Grave (Meir Zarchi, USA, 1978), another rape-revenge film, was only made legally available on video in 2002. The BBFC-certificated version has had approximately seven minutes cut from it – all from the gruelling scenes of the main character's rape. The BBFC's treatment of the scene, Linda Ruth Williams argues, is

> a good example of cuts made with the best intentions skewing the whole film. Also lost along with the more graphic content of the rapes are some images of Jennifer's suffering which in the original version contributed to the justification for her revenge. The less seen of Jennifer's rape the better, one might think; but this may have the curious effect of making the revenge less defensible, since less of the rape is evident. (2002, p70)

Again interpretation is at stake – simply removing some shots does not necessarily make the film more palatable.

Marco Starr's defence of the (uncut) film includes detailed textual analysis of some scenes in order to argue that the film actually damns the perpetrators of the violence rather than provides possible titillation for the viewer:

> To argue that *I Spit on Your Grave* is a dangerously sexist threat towards women simply because it features simulated sexual brutality, is to be unwilling or unable to recognise the importance of the film-maker's own attitudes toward his characters. If anything, it is the men who are actually

being warned to get back in line. The rapists' continuing refusal to recognise Jennifer's rights as a human being make them seem monstrously inhuman; their ultimate deaths can only be viewed as inevitable. (1984, p52)

The case of *Straw Dogs* (Sam Peckinpah, UK, 1971) is interesting because it reveals how including *more* unpleasant material can create the possibility for a more positive reading of the film. Petley (2002) describes how an American cut version of the film (which included a single rape scene in which Susan George's character, Amy, seems to come to enjoy the experience) was continually rejected by the BBFC for video classification:

> Stressing its long-standing concern over 'images which bring sex and violence together', the Board claimed such scenes were potentially 'harmful' if played repeatedly at home. For the BBFC 'Sexual violence may only be shown providing the scenes do not offer sexual thrills'.

However, when the longer British version of the film was submitted in 2001 (which included a second, consecutive and unambiguously unpleasant rape), the Board classified it '18' with no cuts. In this case because the second rape was clearly not something the character welcomed there was no question about the traumatic nature of the event. **Worksheet 9** asks students to study one of the two BBFC reports (Student Notes 1 and 2) on *Straw Dogs* and then to explain the reasons for the different decisions to another group member.

● Religion

Despite the fact that the UK is increasingly secular, religion can still be a potent issue for regulators and audiences. The recent controversy over the BBC's screening of *Jerry Springer: The Opera* (transmitted 8 January 2005) provides some evidence of this. Religious concerns have been on the Board's agenda since 1912 when the first of the only two rules was 'no portrayal of Christ' and in 1916 T P O'Connor's 43 grounds for deletion included: 'the irreverent treatment of sacred objects' and 'materialisation of the conventional figure of Christ'. Representations of Christ continued to be problematic and religious groups exerted pressure when a whiff of blasphemy was detected. In 1979, for example, Mary Whitehouse and Christian group the Festival of Light attempted to provoke public indignation against *Monty Python's Life of Brian* (Terry Jones, UK, 1979), describing it as 'sick, its story veering unsteadily between sadism and sheer silliness' (Dewe Matthews, 1994, p236).

Nearly a decade later, Martin Scorsese's *The Last Temptation of Christ* (USA/Canada, 1988) also proved controversial; the BBFC received 1870 letters and petitions in favour of banning the film on the grounds that Jesus entertains (but rejects) the possibility of retiring and having a sex life. Mary Whitehouse threatened to invoke the blasphemy law if the film warranted it. This was no idle threat; she had successfully brought a private prosecution against *Gay News* in 1977 for publishing a poem depicting Christ's homoerotic attraction to a Roman soldier while on the cross. James Ferman's response to this pressure was to win over a number of priests, deacons and bishops by screening the film to them in the BBFC's viewing room. Although none of them liked the film, 'they were prepared to tell their congregations that Scorsese's liberal retelling of the Gospel was not afflicted by blasphemy' (Dewe Matthews, 1994, p263).

The definition of blasphemy cited in the *Gay News* case was 'any contemptuous reviling, scurrilous or ludicrous matter relating to God, Jesus Christ or the Bible.' It was on this basis that the BBFC refused a certificate to Nigel Wingrove's *Visions of Ecstasy* (UK, 1989), an 18-minute film consisting of only images and music, based on the life and writings of St Theresa of Avila, the 16th-century Carmelite nun. It shows the young St Theresa stabbing her hand, writhing in blood and communion wine and then straddling the crucified body of Christ on the ground, apparently becoming aroused. The BBFC refused a video certificate to the film, but in 1996 Wingrove challenged the decision in the European Commission on Human Rights using Article 10, which states:

> Everyone has the right to freedom of expression. This right shall include freedom to hold opinions and to receive and impart information and ideas without interference by public authority and regardless of frontiers.

The appeal failed because the Commission ruled that, under Article 9, 'respect for the religious feelings of believers can move a state legitimately to restrict the publication of provocative portrayals of objects of religious veneration' and that, therefore, Britain's blasphemy law was valid (Petley and Kermode, 1998, p18). The BBFC's defence of its decision reveals the way in which it engages with the issue of religious representation. It argued to Wingrove:

> The video work submitted by you depicts the mingling of religious ecstasy and sexual passion, a matter which may be of legitimate concern to the artist. It becomes subject to the law of blasphemy, however, if the manner of its presentation is bound to give rise to outrage at the unacceptable treatment of a sacred subject. Because the wounded body of the crucified Christ is presented solely as the focus of, and at certain moments a participant in, the erotic desire of St Theresa, with no attempt to explore the meaning of the imagery beyond engaging the viewer in an erotic experience, it is the Board's view, and that of its legal advisors, that a reasonable jury properly directed would find that the work infringes the criminal law of blasphemy.
> (www.melonfarmers.co.uk/arwingro.htm)

The issue for the Board here was whether it would fall foul of the law by passing the video. Despite the fact that no successful blasphemy prosecution had been brought since the *Gay News* case, it clearly felt that there would have been a case to answer. It is also clear that sexualised images of Christ are particularly problematic – there was considerable controversy, for example, over Madonna's *Like a Prayer* video which featured the singer kissing, bringing to life and passionately embracing the statue of a saint in a church, experiencing stigmata and dancing in front of burning crosses. Images of Christ being brutalised, as in Mel Gibson's *The Passion of the Christ* are, conversely, not seen as derogatory but celebrated for being faithful to the Gospels and representing realistically the physical torment of Jesus' death.

● Class

Richard Falcon (1994, p14) draws our attention to the fact that cinema was censored more strictly than the theatre in the period between the wars. He cites evidence to show that the BBFC viewed the film-going audience as an immature mass, susceptible to demoralisation and, crucially, predominantly comprised of the urban working class. The Board adopted the role of supporter of the status quo and, consequently, cut or banned material depicting 'immorality' (women drinking, for example) and material that might have caused political unrest in the masses (early films by Pudovkin and Eisenstein). Geoffrey Pearson (1984) reveals 'a long and connected history of fearful complaint and controversy' regarding popular entertainment and its putative negative effects on the masses. Similarly, Tom Dewe Matthews, reaching back to Edison's Kinetoscope in the 1890s, argues that the film industry was tainted with a sleazy image and that

> It was the working classes who peered into the little black boxes to see more of 'What the Curate Really Did' and their obvious enjoyment created a mixture of envy and distaste amongst the upper echelons. But there was very little that the 'nicer class of person' could do to curb this instrument of mass appeal. (Dewe Matthews, 1994, p7)

More recently, argues Dewe Matthews,

> ... the censor of the fifties was convinced that middle-class property would be destroyed if working-class youth were allowed to witness – and therefore emulate – Marlon Brando's leather-clad 'leader of the pack' in *The Wild One*. For, then as now, film censorship was not governed by the actual content of the films; it was more concerned with their effect. Thus the censor's long-serving, silently spoken rubric: the larger the audience, the lower the moral resistance to suggestion. (1994, p2)

Or, as Julian Petley suggests,

> In other words, the more popular the cultural form, the more likely it is to be seen by members of the working class, the more heavily its content is likely to be regulated and, if necessary, censored. (1997, p93)

Petley highlights a culturally embedded prejudice against the 'underclass' evident in both the courts and the broadsheet and tabloid press:

The whole attitude is perfectly summed up by the prosecution's famous question at the start of the Lady Chatterley trial in 1960 – 'Is it a book that you would even wish your wife or servants to read?' – but it is often overlooked that an important part of the prosecution's closing speech rested on a quite explicit contrast between the way in which the defence's academic and literary experts would read the book and the way in which 'the ordinary man in the street' would do so. (1997, p93)

Given the nature of this fear and suspicion of this constructed 'Other', Petley argues that:

No one should be in the least surprised, therefore, given the prevalence of such attitudes, that the prospect of unregulated, uncensored videos being freely available to the British public at the start of the 1980s was greeted with such horror and dismay from certain quarters, and that draconian censorship was soon imposed. (1997, p93)

The idea that class prejudice underpins contemporary decision-making about cutting or refusing certification is denied by the BBFC, but it has been cited as a determinant in some recent cases. Kevin Maher suggests that Gasper Noé's *Irreversible* was given preferential treatment by the BBFC because of its European 'arthouse' orientation:

... The blatant trickery of the arthouse auteurs and their questionable celebration of extreme screen violence is ultimately culturally acceptable where the likes of Tarantino never had a chance. Noé may sicken stomachs and smash heads with the best of them, but when he writes in his director's notes that the formal concept for *Irreversible* begins with the notion that 'time reveals everything. It only exists within us and we through it', he is appealing to the deep-rooted intellectual snobbery that controls the arbitrary line between vapid American movies and precious cinéma d'art. He is appealing to the Pavlovian response in all of us that salivates at the sight of cinema subtitles as if they confer some integrity on the film that appears above them. Thus the BBFC have released Noé's film without cuts while simultaneously agonising over the rating on *Spider-Man*. (2003)

A similar interpretation is possible of the BBFC's treatment of Wes Craven's *The Last House on the Left*, which has only recently been awarded a video certificate following cuts. Mark Kermode, describing the conflict between the BBFC and the UK distributor of the film, Blue Underground, indicates that

at the centre of the furore are the apparent randomness of the BBFC's attitude to graphic depictions of sexual violence and the suggestion that it is more lenient towards subtitled (or 'arthouse') fare. (Kermode, 2001, p26)

He cites Pasolini's *Saló* (Italy/France, 1975) and Virginie Despentes' *Baise-moi* as examples of European films which seem to have received a lighter touch than *The Last House on the Left*:

Pasolini's *Saló*, in which victims are stripped, raped, whipped and forced to eat excrement for a large part of the film's running time, was recently passed uncut under the strict provisions of the Video Recordings Act (VRA). For the cinema release of *Baise-moi*, which like *The Last House on the Left* has a rape-revenge narrative, a single 10-second close-up of vaginal penetration was removed from a lengthy rape sequence which otherwise retains its explicit depiction of sexual violation and humiliation. Although *The Last House on the Left* contains no such hardcore sexual imagery, and its scenes of sexual humiliation are cumulatively shorter than those in *Saló*, the BBFC has demanded that approximately nine times as much material be removed from Craven's film as from *Baise-moi* before cinema classification can be considered. (Kermode, 2001, p26)

Julian Petley raises the issue in an interview with former BBFC Director Robin Duval, who explains and defends the Board's treatment of different kinds of potentially controversial material:

JP: The Annual Report 1999 ... states: 'whether or not something is acceptable still depends ultimately upon how it is treated ie its context.' Doesn't this offer ammunition to those who accuse the board of being softer on arthouse than on commercial movies?

RD: It was difficult to combat this argument as long as all the films that posed a challenge to our guidelines were non-English language movies and therefore almost by definition arthouse – until Patrice Chéreau's *Intimacy* turned up earlier this year. Of course we applied exactly the same criteria to *Intimacy* as we would to anything else, and lo and behold we passed uncut an English-speaking movie with the same kind of content which people thought had been reserved for such arthouse work as *Ai No Corrida*, *Romance* and *The Idiots*. But now we're told that *Intimacy* is a British arthouse movie. You can't win – but nor do we expect to. So we're sitting waiting for a popular movie that sets identical challenges, and we will treat that exactly the same. If it's a movie which within its own internal context justifies something unprecedented, then it's possible we'd take a liberal view of that. (Petley, 2001, p31)

The key question here is whether there are legitimate grounds for arguing that some kind of class bias obtains in the BBFC decision-making process. The evidence that Kermode cites, although persuasive, is not conclusive because the examples are not identical and, although his descriptions of *Saló* sound shocking and his reference to the *quantities* of sexual humiliation in (and cut from) each film seem to highlight an injustice in their differing treatment, we should notice that this is the same kind of rhetoric which is used to persuade readers of popular newspapers that films they haven't seen should be banned. In this case:

... the BBFC remains adamant that there is no comparison to be made between *The Last House on the Left* and *Baise-moi* or *Saló*, and therefore no case for claiming 'precedent'. According to [Sue] Clark [BBFC Head of Press and Publicity], 'It is important to point out the difference in the nature of the violence being presented. *The Last House on the Left* contains three graphic rape scenes involving knives used on naked women: stripping a woman at knife-point, disembowelling a woman after raping her and knife cuts to a woman's chest during rape. The single rape scene in *Baise-moi* contains no weapons, but was cut nevertheless, and the violence in *Saló* does not contain this level of graphic and bloody violence.' (Kermode, 2001, p26)

Any debate around possible class bias, therefore, must acknowledge the need to identify differing treatments of directly comparable examples – we must compare like with like. This, of course, does not approach the question of whether bits should be cut from these films in the first place and also, given that we only get to see them in a cut form, it is difficult to make concrete comparative judgements about what has been excised. However, students can work with examples of 'arthouse' and commercial films that have some common story and action elements and discuss the respective certificates given and the possible reasons for this. A comparison between, say, *Boyz N the Hood* (John Singleton, USA, 1991) or *Juice* (Ernest Dickerson, USA, 1992) and *La Haine* (Mathieu Kassovitz, France, 1995), can generate some debate around these issues.

Worksheet 10 is designed to get students to identify any comparable depictions of violence, examples of drug use and instances of 'bad' language in order to make certification decisions (all received '15' certificates for theatrical release and on video). It is possible that *La Haine* will emerge as a film requiring a different assessment because it is in French, subtitled and in black and white. Some students in the past have argued that the film should probably be rated '18' in terms of content, but that these elements are 'neutralised' by its auteurist

trappings and, in any case, younger people are unlikely to be attracted by it. This provides opportunities to discuss assumptions about:

- The 'quality' of the film
- The likely audience
- The competence of that audience to process it.

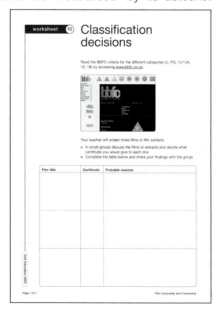

To access student worksheets and other online materials go to *Teaching Film Censorship and Controversy* at **www.bfi.org.uk/tfms** and enter User name: **filmcens@bfi.org.uk** and Password: **te1908ce.**

It is probably naïve to assume that these factors play no part in a BBFC examiner's assessment of a particular film, and therefore these are useful questions to ask. James Ferman's comment on *Funny Games* (Michael Haneke, Austria, 1997) is revealing of a particular perspective on the audience:

> It's an Austrian film with subtitles about a middle-class family being under assault and in a sense it's a self-selecting audience, and I think probably we felt that the people that might get off on the movie in the wrong way probably wouldn't find their way into it. But who knows? There could be some dangerous characters around who happen to like German movies. (*The Last Days of the Board*, 1999)

Barker et al (2001) describe the Board's decision to pass Catherine Breillat's *Romance,*

> with its clearly seen male and female genitalia and its scenes of fellatio and sado-masochism, on the grounds that it was so clearly an 'arthouse' film, would be subtitled, and therefore could be safely permitted. (p143)

He suggest that this provides more evidence of a distinction being created between 'ordinary vulnerable viewers' and 'sophisticated secure viewers'.

- **Language (see Case study 3)**

- **Shock**

The concept of shock often goes hand in hand with discussions of censorship and controversy, but not always and not inevitably. It is useful to examine the meaning of the term – is it simply an extreme form of surprise or is it fundamentally different in nature? An early exercise with students is useful to try to identify the reasons why something they have seen in the cinema or on television has shocked them, or why they perceive it to have the potential to shock others. Subsequently it should be possible to categorise different types of shock.

See **Worksheet 11**.

To access student worksheets and other online materials go to *Teaching Film Censorship and Controversy* at **www.bfi.org.uk/tfms** and enter User name: **filmcens@bfi.org.uk** and Password: **te1908ce**.

worksheet 11 The nature of shock

In small groups discuss the following:
- What do you think the word 'shock' means? Write your definitions below.

Individually:
- Think of something you have seen in the cinema, on television or on video/DVD that has shocked you. Why did it shock you?
- Complete the table below with your shocking event and your reason.
- Interview two other people about a media event that has shocked them. Make notes in the table below.

Shocking event on film/TV/video	Reason why it was found shocking
Self	
Person 1	
Person 2	

- Look at the reasons. Do they have anything in common? What sorts of things do people find shocking?

Graphic shock

It might be possible even at this stage to start to identify categories of shock – students are most likely to identify visual or graphic shock, such as images of evisceration and mutilation. Linda Ruth Williams in a discussion of the power of filmic images of the violation of the eye suggests, in relation to *Un Chien andalou* (Luis Buñuel and Salvador Dali, France, 1928), why they might be so shocking:

> 'Once upon a time', we are told, a man sharpens his cutthroat razor. We see his hands purposefully perform the task, his intent face as he tests the blade on his thumb. The man goes to the balcony and watches a cloud move towards the full moon; a woman's eye is held wide open. The cloud crosses the moon; the razor passes across the eyeball, slitting it open, right there on screen, and liquid oozes out. This opening two minutes of Buñuel's *Un Chien andalou* (1928) is one of the most shocking sequences in cinema history. No one struggles, there is no apparent pain or flinching, the act is as dispassionate as it is grotesque. Victim and aggressor seem entirely inappropriate terms of judgement; certainly one person is injured while another wields a razor, but it is perhaps the viewer who occupies the most painful position. What taboos are violated in this spectacle, what tensions are released? What is at stake in showing the obscene act, which ought to be kept to the margins between cuts? (1994, p14)

See **Worksheet 12**.

To access student worksheets and other online materials go to *Teaching Film Censorship and Controversy* at **www.bfi.org.uk/tfms** and enter User name: **filmcens@bfi.org.uk** and Password: **te1908ce**.

William identifies two points at work in the film: one is the spectacle of violation of the human body, the other is an attitude within the film towards violence, shared by perpetrator and recipient. A screening of the film and some follow-up questions might elicit student responses which acknowledge this and enable you to redefine or reconfirm the categories of shock that you have arrived at with the students; it should be possible at least to argue for the existence of a category that depends upon the image – an assault on the eye of the viewer perhaps. In addition, it should be possible to propose a category of shock that depends upon some kind of ideological disturbance, in this case the unfathomable absence of emotion and resistance – a shocking concept.

Reference to contextual factors can also be an illuminating approach to the concept of shock. In the case of *Un Chien andalou*, it is possible to argue that the shocking scene which inaugurates the film becomes less powerful as the film develops its strategy of 'not making sense' and offering the viewer surreal and absurd images, to which an immediate response may be laughter. In the context of a film concerned with portraying such a deliberately fantastic and 'unrealistic' representation of a 'world', it may be that the ideological shock of the scene is lessened retrospectively. It would be possible to put this to the test by screening only the first scene, getting responses to it, then screening the whole film and asking similar questions to see if the 'shocked responses' had changed. A second screening of the film could also elicit responses to the proposal that shock may depend to a degree upon novelty – is the eyeball slicing scene as shocking the second or third time around? It may still be grotesque (especially when we realise that it is in fact a cow's eyeball that is being sliced open and not the girl's), but is it *shocking*?

Ideological shock

The notion of 'ideological shock' may be hard to pin down, but it could be defined as a shock to the 'sensibilities' of the viewer – sensibilities which are not merely personal, but informed by the dominant moral and ethical structures of the culture (and subcultures) they inhabit. We are talking then about a shock to value systems, which in contemporary Western culture could apply to depictions of racism, misogyny and abuse of various kinds. Neil LaBute's *In the Company of Men* (USA, 1997), one could argue, depicts a shockingly cruel manipulation of a deaf female colleague by two men and incorporates a particularly shocking moment when one of the protagonists (Chad, played by Aaron Eckhart) reveals to his 'friend' (Howard, played by Matt Malloy) that he has been cruelly and cynically manipulating both of them simply for the pleasure of causing emotional distress. In Todd Solondz's *Happiness* (USA, 1998), although we do not witness the act (which would entail the sort of graphic shock we witness in Tim Roth's *The War Zone*, UK/Italy, 1998), we learn that a respectable middle-class therapist is a paedophile and that he has drugged and raped one of his son's school friends.

Thomas Vinterberg's *Festen* (Denmark, 1998) has at its heart a scene in which a grownup son (Christian, played by Ulrich Thomsen) gives a speech to a celebratory audience at his father's birthday party. The tone of the event is dramatically subverted when Christian reveals the abuse suffered by him and his sister at the hands of their father. Richard Falcon describes this as 'involving the audience in a life-altering shift of perspective ... [which] enacts the social theatre of shock and embarrassment to wonderfully comic and dramatic effect.' (Falcon, 1998, p 11)

A contemporary audience might find the casual racist taunts embodied in 1970s' TV sitcoms such as *Love Thy Neighbour* (ITV, 1972–76) and *'Til Death Us Do Part* (BBC, 1972–5) shocking because they break current taboos. Gaspar Noé, the director of such extreme films as *Seul contre tous* (France, 1998) and *Irreversible*,

> ... says that he has rarely been shocked by cinema – but was when a lightweight French television comedy show invited National Front leader Jean-Marie le Pen on to crack jokes. (Falcon, 1999, p13)

Narrative/textual shock

Another category of shock which may be elicited through discussion is that of narrative shock. This may be defined as an extreme event which causes the viewer to feel as if some kind of contract or agreement between him/her and the text has been broken. An obvious example is the murder of Marion Crane in *Psycho* (Alfred Hitchcock, USA, 1960). The film establishes her as the protagonist, encourages us to invest in her emotionally and then violently dispatches her within the first hour. Another example of this kind of shock is from the television series *Spooks* (BBC1, 2002–), in which, in the second episode, one of the lead characters (Helen, played by Lisa Faulkner) has her head plunged into a deep-fat fryer and is then shot. Apparently, according to the 334 viewers who complained, this was one of the most shocking deaths ever depicted in TV fiction. The show's producer attempts to account for this effect:

> Given how many people are routinely killed off in the course of an average evening's viewing, it's worth analysing for a moment quite why this scene had the impact it did. Was it the graphic nature of the violence? Well, not really, because the worst of the action took place off camera. Sound, editing and the viewers' imaginations did the rest. Was the violence unannounced, and therefore a surprise? Not really, once again. Not only was there a clear warning before the programme began, but for anyone who missed that, the subject matter of the episode (a conspiracy to stir up inter-racial violence perpetrated by a man who clearly beat his wife) was hardly the stuff of which chirpy little bucolic fantasies are made. No, what seems really to have shocked people is that *Spooks* turned their expectations upside down. It ambushed the

audience by doing what television almost never does. In brutal fashion *Spooks* killed off one of its leads in the second episode of a long-running series. No one is going to wake up after a nightmare, Helen doesn't have a twin sister, Lisa Faulkner simply isn't coming back. And in mainstream TV series you just don't do that. (Garrett, 2002)

This seems to get to the heart of this thing we could call 'narrative shock'. Generically it would have been more predictable for one of the other characters to overthrow the villains, or for a crack team to suddenly break in and save the day, so the event fundamentally shook viewers' expectations of the story and dramatically broke the contract between viewer and text which implies that, in a television series, the lead characters are going to appear week after week. There is a similar contract present between the audience and a feature film, agreeing that the 'hero' will undergo a series of experiences and emerge at the end changed in some way in order to repay our investment in them. The statement above also makes it clear that, like *Psycho*, in which 'the horror resides less in the actual images than in their summary implication' (Clover, 1992, p41), the essence of the shock does not necessarily lie in the graphic depiction of violence.

It is useful to examine examples of the sort of shocking effect which is constructed through the 'machinery of representation' rather than 'content', such as a key moment in *A Room for Romeo Brass* (Shane Meadows, UK/Canada, 1999). The scene, about 35 minutes into the film, suddenly reveals a dark side to Paddy Considine's Morrell, whom we have hitherto seen as a romantic buffoon, the naïve butt of the two boys' (Knocks and Romeo) practical jokes and a character whose heart is essentially in the right place. It is this sudden revelation of character which makes the moment shocking; initially Morrell is good-naturedly prodding Knocks into admitting that a joke at his expense was intentional and, when Knocks reluctantly concedes, Morrell explodes into spitting fury, grabbing the boy by the scruff of the neck, pulling a knife on him and unleashing a torrent of abuse and threats. True, the verbal content is unpleasant (albeit in a grossly exaggerated, almost juvenile way), especially when Morrell promises not only to avenge himself on Knocks personally but also to kill his family, but the shock effect results from the contrast between the monster who appears on screen and the harmless fool we thought we knew. This effect is accentuated by the shift from single shots, in which each participant has plenty of space around them, to a cramped and claustrophobic two-shot in which Morrell's snarling mouth is in the centre of the frame, his eyes partially hidden by the peak of his cap, and Knocks' discomfort is made tangible by his pale face being squeezed into the bottom corner of the frame.

There will probably be some debate around the relationship between shock and surprise. The above example certainly has an element of surprise, in that it is unexpected. However, there is a difference between the two concepts which may be more than a difference of degree. This difference can be explored through comparing and contrasting this example with some generic examples of surprising moments from horror or thriller films, such as *Halloween* (John Carpenter, USA, 1978). **Worksheet 13** invites an analysis of such moments (any appropriate examples can be used), which will probably benefit from being seen in the context of the narrative, and asks students to differentiate between those which are merely surprising (and, perhaps, predictable within specific generic limitations) and those which constitute some kind of profound emotional disruption. It may be useful at this point to invoke Japanese director Takeshi Kitano's take on shock – when asked about the influences on his depictions of violence he offers this perspective:

> ... one of the scenes which influenced me, or impressed me most, was a scene on TV where a South Vietnamese soldier put a gun to the head of a Viet Cong and killed him. That was the most shocking and impressive scene ... There was nothing, then, suddenly, in the quietness of everything, a man kills – that is the impression of violence that I try to catch again in my films. (Kennedy, 2001, p87)

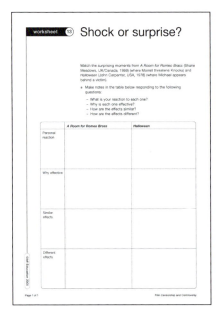

To access student worksheets and other online materials go to *Teaching Film Censorship and Controversy* at **www.bfi.org.uk/tfms** and enter User name: **filmcens@bfi.org.uk** and Password: **te1908ce**.

Clearly there is an element of surprise here – the eruption of something into the 'quietness' – but there is also something profoundly disturbing about the scene, which may bring us back to the eyeball-slicing in *Un Chien andalou* – the casual violation of another human being, the lack of emotion – only here we are seeing a sign of an actual killing which makes it even more shocking. Kitano also suggests that 'comedy and violence share common aspects; both are unexpected, you can't anticipate them', perhaps making it possible to invoke the Aristotelian notion of the *peripeteia* – the sudden reversal of fortune, the element of surprise or wonder, the tragic recognition that one is holding the 'wrong end of a stick' – that some (Palmer, 1987) have related to the punch line in a joke. The accidental shooting of Marvin in *Pulp Fiction* provides a useful example in debating the relationship between notionally shocking violence and comedy.

Shock as a cultural phenomenon

We have seen how the study of censorship benefits from a historical perspective, which reveals the contingent and contextual dependency of decisions to certify, cut and ban. A similar approach to the notion of shocking cinema can be just as revealing. Kim Newman's article, 'The 10 Most Shocking Moments in Cinema History', is prefaced with the comment 'If you look back over the cinematic century, the scenes which stirred up trouble look rather tame today ...' and his selective list (with paraphrased comments) may provide some historical illumination of the notion of shock.

> **Film**: *L'Arrivée d'un train en gare de la ciotat* (Lumière Brothers, France, 1895)
> **Reason for shock**: Audiences, unfamiliar with the new technology of projected moving images, apparently panicked at the sight of a full-size train roaring silently towards them.
>
> **Film**: *Un Chien andalou* (Luis Buñuel and Salvador Dali, France, 1928)
> **Reason for shock**: Audiences, then and now, shudder – eye abuse is infallibly cringe-inducing.
>
> **Film**: *Frankenstein* (James Whale, USA, 1931)
> **Reason for shock**: The monster drowns a little girl – considered so shocking that it was cut from prints of the film for 60 years. (Child murder remains one the great taboos of the movies.)
>
> **Film**: *The Wild One* (Laslo Benedek, USA, 1953)
> **Reason for shock**: Fear that attitude of Brando's biker Johnny might encourage teenage violence led to the film being banned in Britain for 20 years.
>
> **Film**: *Who's Afraid of Virginia Woolf?* (Mike Nichols, USA, 1966)
> **Reason for shock**: Language – Elizabeth Taylor says 'shit'.
>
> **Film**: *Blow-Up* (Michaelangelo Antonioni, UK/Italy, 1966)
> **Reason for shock**: Sex – David Hemming's photographer has sex with two girls after a photo session, causing moral outrage in *The Daily Mail*.
>
> **Film**: *Sunday, Bloody Sunday* (John Schlesinger, UK, 1971)
> **Reason for shock**: Sexuality – there is an affectionate kiss between Peter Finch's middle-aged man and his younger male lover.
>
> **Film**: *Straw Dogs* (Sam Peckinpah, UK, 1971)
> **Reason for shock**: Sexual violence – Susan George's character appears to take pleasure in being raped.

Film: *Last Tango in Paris* (Bernardo Bertolucci, France/Italy, 1972)
Reason for shock: Sex – Marlon Brando's character sodomises Maria Schneider's character on the floor of a Paris apartment.

Film: *Reservoir Dogs* (Quentin Tarantino, USA, 1992)
Reason for shock: Sadistic violence – Michael Madsen's Mr Blonde, while shimmying to a 1970s' hit by Stealer's Wheel, sadistically cuts off the ear of a captive policeman.

(Newman, 2001)

Playing illustrative clips from some of these films and using a follow-up exercise should provide some revealing insights into the nature of shock; it is likely that students will be amused by the notion that *The Wild One* had the power to shock some of its audience and should appreciate the dependency of the response upon a specific time. Similarly the taboo language used in *Who's Afraid of Virginia Woolf?* will seem very tame to a contemporary audience and some historical contextual information about audience expectations will be useful for students.

See **Worksheet 14**.

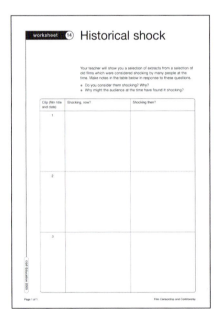

To access student worksheets and other online materials go to *Teaching Film Censorship and Controversy* at **www.bfi.org.uk/tfms** and enter User name: **filmcens@bfi.org.uk** and Password: **te1908ce**.

Discussions on the nature of shock in moving image texts will probably refer to a range of determining factors. It might be argued that shock is the consequence of the intersection of specific factors that might include age, gender, social/cultural experience, media literacy, historical context. With reference to one of the historical examples cited above, a useful exercise would be to identify the nature of the factors, the conjunction of which produced shock for particular audiences. What will become evident is the fact that shock is always contingent and, therefore, not simply attributable to particular textual qualities – it is unlikely that contemporary students will respond to a 1970s' text in the same way as its audience at the time and it is useful to register this fact. However, it is worth testing whether the boundaries have shifted significantly in all respects; the ability to tolerate greater degrees of 'bad language', sex and violence may have increased, but if it's true that the eyeball-slicing scene in *Un Chien andalou* is still 'infallibly cringe-inducing', this indicates that there may be some violations which approach universality. Perhaps this is too lofty a claim; it may be that we are still only recognising taboos which are currently valid. It is also the case that it seems easier for some boundaries to be shifted than others. It may be possible, for example, to break linguistic taboos through repetition of the offending words (a concept the comedian Lenny Bruce attempted to demonstrate through some of his material on racist and sexual taboo words), but representations of sexual violence are not defused by time or repetition so easily.

Worksheet 15 is designed to illustrate diagrammatically how the intersection of specific factors may produce the phenomenon of shock. When the exercise is completed for a specific film there should be the potential for debate around whether the factors are all equally weighted, if they all need to be present in order for the shock phenomenon to occur, and the degree to which it is necessary to account for individual experience in determining whether something is shocking.

To access student worksheets and other online materials go to *Teaching Film Censorship and Controversy* at **www.bfi.org.uk/tfms** and enter User name: **filmcens@bfi.org.uk** and Password: **te1908ce**.

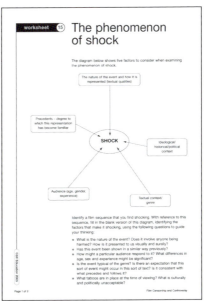

1 of 2 pages

A degree of conjecture about 'other' audiences (in terms of generation, class or historical moment) can be involved for this exercise, although stereotypes and pejorative judgements should be challenged. The exercise may give rise to some interesting results: historical texts may still have the power to shock. It may also be useful to include texts which were not necessarily shocking at the time (such as the sitcom examples cited above), but which may elicit shocked responses now. It might also be worth considering what to call the response if not all of the factors to cause 'shock' are in place; 'revulsion' and 'disgust' may be cited as possible alternatives, as might 'surprise' or 'satisfaction'. In any case it is worth assessing the responses comparatively to try to identify whether these things are related to shock or whether they belong to a different category altogether. Is the sight, for example, of Divine eating fresh dog faeces (in a single, unedited shot) in John Waters' *Pink Flamingos* (USA, 1972) shocking or simply revolting? Does it disturb the mind or merely the stomach?

Case Studies

3

Case study 1: Violence

Focus film: *Funny Games* (Michael Haneke, Austria, 1997)

Funny Games could be described as a thriller. A middle-class family on holiday are visited by two well-spoken, polite young men who prove to be psychopaths and who subsequently psychologically and physically torture the family, ultimately killing them all. Jonathan Romney explains some of the reasons why this is an interesting case study for screen violence:

Funny Games

> Haneke's film is not just about acts of terrorism – it is itself a terrorist attack on the viewer. And, according to Haneke, the assault is for our own good ... Whatever horrors happen on screen – or rather, off screen – it's always with a chilling aside to us. *Funny Games* takes us beyond cinematic voyeurism: it coerces us into being complicit too ... the audience can no longer stand back from the events, but is deeply implicated in them. In a sense, [Haneke]'s concerned to trap us into admitting how much violence we can stand to see. As the director puts it, 'Anyone who leaves doesn't need the film, anyone who stays does.' Horrified by what he sees in mainstream cinema, Haneke – very much a moralist – sets out to cure the malaise by making us stare it in the face, under the cold light of laboratory conditions.
>
> ... Haneke is not the first film-maker to point out that we have become inured to screen violence and that it is our own sadism that we see being vented on screen. Much the same points are made, in a similarly self-conscious way, by commercial horror films such as Wes Craven's *Scream*. But where such films tend to make the point with self-ironising

humour, softening the blow and leaving us wanting more, Haneke refuses any such relief. ... It's only when the film is over and we have recovered our wits that we can start to question the effectiveness of Haneke's approach. (2001)

Here is a film, then, with a specific extra-textual agenda – Haneke presents us with representations of violence which deny the audience their usual 'pleasures'. Most of the on-screen violence is 'psychological' as the two young men toy with their captives, betting them that they will be dead in 12 hours' time. Most of the physical violence is off screen and represented through sound effects – the killing of the family dog and the murder of the son, for example. This device can be usefully discussed in the context of shock; there is something profoundly unsettling about knowing that an act of violence is taking place whilst being denied the 'visual gratification' that usually accompanies it.

The film uses certain 'alienation' techniques which, perhaps in a Brechtian way, require the audience to focus on the 'message'. One example of this is the manipulation of time when the mother grabs the gun and shoots one of the young men. The other exclaims, hunts for the TV remote and then rewinds the scene, resurrecting his companion. When the mother reaches for the gun again he intercepts her. Without the manipulation of time this would be a 'crowd pleasing moment' (Haneke has said that the Cannes audience applauded at this point), but this film is a polemic against the pleasures of violent entertainment so the moment is literally taken back. Another device which has a similar effect occurs regularly in the film and entails one of the young men, Paul, directly addressing the audience, making us complicit in his 'game' and breaking the realist illusion. This is most chilling at the end of the film when he visits another house to 'borrow some eggs' and his expression to camera reveals that he is intending to start the whole process of intimidation and torture again.

In an interview with Haneke, Trevor Johnston (2001) asks him:

And the ... moment where you rewind the film, that's the prime example of making the audience realise how open they are to manipulation?
MH: Yes, but there are various devices in the film which highlight the audience's awareness of their status as consumers of violence. Where the characters turn to the camera and break the illusion, for instance, or the bit where they talk about being within the length of a feature film. Another thing that happens is where we break some of the basic conventions of the thriller genre, the understanding that no animals or children will be harmed. As a result, what you expect of a thriller is broken down, and that's obviously another form of alienation.
TJ: You keep a lot of the violence off screen too, which also works against the expectations of today's viewers ...
MH: Well I can't stand in a glass house and throw stones. If I'm polemicising against violent entertainment, I have to see how I can do that without falling into the same trap. The important issue is actually the

representation of violence, so I have to find a means of representation which doesn't have that obscene quality of the representations of violence I'm polemicising against.

TJ: But is the representation of violence on the screen or is it the construct that the viewers assemble in their imagination? Particularly in a film which uses sound and the off-screen space in such a suggestive way as this, it's possible that we can actually imagine we've seen more horrible things than have strictly appeared within the frame …

MH: Of course, every intelligent film works with the fantasy of the audience.

TJ: Well, in Britain at least there was a lot of a fuss over the ear-slicing scene in *Reservoir Dogs*, which was another suggestive sequence where you didn't see very much but it still managed to upset a lot of people. Do you think *Funny Games* could prompt the same debate?

MH: The question is about the way the audience is involved in violence but without experiencing any sense of guilt. The cinema of violence lives for this sense of being involved in watching violence without any sense of guilt about that process.

Confirming this standpoint, Richard Falcon says of Haneke,

> This is what he called his anti-Tarantino film. It's a film which removes humour from the representation of violence. It's a film that wants to reach out and make you feel this vicarious violence, but it's also a provocation that puts you on the spot – 'Do I stay or do I leave?' that's the moment at which this film comes alive. (The Last Days of the Board, 1999)

This is what makes *Funny Games* both provocative and useful from an academic point of view: Does it 'mean' what Haneke wants it to mean? Are the off-screen representations of violence any less horrifying or shocking? Isn't being horrified by a film a form of being entertained? All these questions start to unpick the complex relationship between text and audience and Haneke's experiments with mode of address and technique can provide some excellent, if disturbing, stimuli.

Case study 2: Sexual violence

Focus film: *Irreversible* (Gaspar Noé, France, 2002)

Like *Funny Games*, *Irreversible* is a difficult film to watch because it is concerned with representations of violence on screen and uses distanciation techniques to get us to focus on the nature of violence. These techniques include a reverse narrative structure, dizzying mobile camera work, use of (apparently) unbroken takes for each of the 12 sequences and, in its central sequence, a static ground-level shot. Unlike *Funny Games*, *Irreversible* puts its violence firmly on screen and makes it into spectacle.

Arguably, the reverse narrative decontextualises the brutal head-smashing scene at the beginning of the film and therefore makes it impossible for the audience to 'enjoy' it or even understand it as revenge. This fact alone highlights one of the factors determining the 'meaning' of violence on screen. The issues around *Irreversible* involve disagreements

Irreversible

about what it 'says' and how it says it. Nick James (James and Kermode, 2003) argues that it is an exercise in shock and that it

> disorients the viewer with avant-garde camera moves and subaural noise as a preparation for the horror it's about to present. This amounts to two unendurable scenes – one of extreme violent revenge, the other of graphically realistic rape and violence.

James is repelled by these scenes, and the way in which Monica Bellucci's Alex is sexualised, but criticises the film chiefly because its shock tactics are in the service of a banal philosophy. In addition,

> The primary emotion *Irreversible* plays on is fear of the streets, and in that sense it's as repressive a text as tabloid newspapers which exaggerate crimes, or programmes like *Crimewatch UK* which feed urban paranoia.

Kermode (James and Kermode, 2003), on the other hand, calls the film

> a bravura slice of exploitation cinema that exists at least in part to batter the viewer into awed submission, its roots based in the grind-house markets forged by such 1970s', American slashers as *The Last House on the Left* (a film whose tagline dared the audience 'to avoid fainting').

Kermode is impressed by Noé's achievement of profound visceral effects on the viewer

> without resort to cruelty to animals, mondo 'reality' footage of documentary death and suffering or even censorably explicit images of actual human sexual activity

and argues that this cross-pollination of *Straw Dogs* and *Memento* (Christopher Nolan, USA, 2000) results in a neat deconstruction of the rape–revenge narrative, laying bare its prejudices. Kermode also validates the construction of the rape scene:

> Crucially Noé goes out of his way to depict rape as an act of violence rather than of sex, unlike in many more mainstream depictions of such assaults ... When I looked away, I did so not in disgust but in horror; unable to watch (as indeed one should be), but certain of the justification of the display.

He concludes that *Irreversible* is a film which attempts to knock you out, literally, but in doing so also achieves a level of artistic honesty that belies its base motives.

For James then, the film is shock with nothing to say and with a sexualised victim if, not a sexualised rape. For Kermode, it is the film's construction of visceral horror which is its achievement, as well as its unflinching portrayal of the horror of sexual violence.

Case study 3: Language

Focus film: *Sweet Sixteen* (Ken Loach, UK/Germany/Spain/France/Italy, 2002)

Although a fairly modest example in the context of some of the other films mentioned in this guide, *Sweet Sixteen* has been the subject of considerable controversy, fuelled by its director. It tells the story of 15-year-old Liam who wants to provide a place for him and his mother to live when she gets out of prison, and get her away from her violent, drug-dealing boyfriend Stan. Consequently

Sweet Sixteen

Liam steals Stan's drugs and sets up as a dealer with his best friend until a local gangster realises what he's doing and takes him on as a runner. When his mother is released she goes back to Stan and, on his 16th birthday, Liam argues with Stan and stabs him.

The controversy over this film is driven by the fact that the BBFC gave it an '18' certificate, despite the fact that it deals with young people, their relationships with each other and adults, and the moral choices they make. The reason given was the use of swearing in the film, as the film's scriptwriter Paul Laverty (2002) explains: 'The British Board of Film Classification ... has been troubled by the rough language, especially the "aggressive" use of the word "cunt", in Ken Loach's new film *Sweet Sixteen*.' Laverty goes on to explain that extensive research prior to writing the film showed him that young people who had seen other Loach films 'recognised their own world reflected back at them via the story and the dilemma of the characters, principally because of the language we used'. He also uses a scene from his and Loach's previous film, *My Name Is Joe* (UK/Germany, 1998), to question whether the mere presence of this word is as significant as the Board seems to think:

There is a scene at the end of *My Name Is Joe* when the main character torments and insults the young lad just prior to his suicide. It is dark and vicious, but I suppose more by luck than intent he doesn't use the word 'cunt'. Certainly the scene is as aggressive and disturbing as any of the scenes where 'cunt' is used in *Sweet Sixteen*. With all due respect, I think this example demonstrates the great danger in an overly microscopic examination of the specific word.

The Board's guidelines at '15' say that

> There may be frequent use of strong language; the strongest terms (eg 'cunt') are only rarely acceptable. Continued aggressive use of strong language and sexual abuse is unacceptable.

The use of the term in the film is aggressive, and at its most unpleasant when Stan's fury at Liam's refusal to smuggle drugs into his mother's prison boils over, but as Laverty argues:

> We have tried to be true to what we have found ... the very least we can do is be loyal to their predicament. And the very least I could do as a writer, was to be true to how they speak. Are they now to be denied the right to hear themselves speak in the cinemas?

Fuelling the controversy, Loach urged teenagers to go and see the film, whether or not they were over 18, and this led to the inevitable BBC Radio 4 *Today* programme debate:

> Conservative MP Peter Bottomley – a former chairman of Children's Society – came out in support of the BBFC when he told BBC Radio 4's *Today* programme on Friday that bad language was not necessary. 'I suspect Ken Loach could have got everything across that he wanted without having more than one Pygmalion moment,' Mr Bottomley said. But Loach told the programme it would be 'silly' for the characters in his film not to use strong language. 'If you are to be true to the story, it would be silly for them to say, "Oh blow, dear me,"' he said. 'The problem is that the censors live in their own little ivory tower and are playing to their own middle-class gallery.' (BBC Online, 2002)

Laverty too suspects some form of class prejudice at work:

> It is now certain that the 15-, 16- and 17-year-olds – and many who were much younger – who shared their lives with us in preparation for this film will not be allowed to see *Sweet Sixteen* in a cinema by law. Is it important? I think it is. I believe it is censorship and I suspect, since it is impossible to prove, 'class' prejudice suffuses the decision, the guidelines and the whole bloody apple cart. (2002)

As a result of this controversy Robin Duval, shortly before retiring as Director of the Board, decided to conduct a review of its policy on swearing (Travis, 2004). The key question here is which sorts of language in which contexts require which sort of regulation?

Case study 4: Press controversy

Focus film: *Crash* (David Cronenberg, Canada, 1996)

The reception of David Cronenberg's *Crash* in the UK provides us with an excellent example of how the press can attempt to generate a moral panic. The vitriolic campaign, started by *The Evening Standard* and picked up by its Associated Newspapers stablemate *The Daily Mail*, sought to get the film banned by the BBFC. The papers' failure to do this may indicate that there had been a change in the

Crash

general climate since the last press-fuelled panic about films and their effects in 1993. Nevertheless, as a direct or indirect result of the campaign, Westminster Council banned *Crash* after the BBFC passed it uncut in March 1997, and the then Heritage Secretary Virginia Bottomley was apparently keen for other councils to do the same. The fact that neighbouring councils, Kensington and Chelsea, and Camden, accepted the BBFC's classification rather undermined Westminster's defiant posture, as the film was able to open in the West End.

Barker et al (2001) argue that *The Daily Mail*'s attacks on the film shaped the way that the film was dealt with by all reviewers, and analyse the way in which it set the agenda or 'terrain of debate'. The campaign started with a review in *The Evening Standard* by Alexander Walker in June 1996 who described the film as containing 'some of the most perverted acts and theories of sexual deviance I have ever seen propagated in main-line cinema'. Kermode and Petley (1997) draw attention to the 'juicy headline' for the article – 'A movie beyond the bounds of depravity' – a phrase which would be 'recycled endlessly over the next few months, whenever *Crash* was mentioned in print'. They quote Cronenberg, who argued:

> "I ... think, incidentally, that that phrase actually means my movie is not depraved, because if you're 'beyond the bounds of depravity' then you are by definition someplace else, and I certainly thought the film was someplace else.' (1997, p6)

This logic and rationality was not to be a feature of the anti-*Crash* campaign which was built on hyperbole and metaphors of disease, disaster and decay. Barker et al note that almost all subsequent references to Walker's 'perverted acts and theories' statement missed out the words 'and theories', which attribute some of the film's impact to a cognitive response; subsequent reviews of the film were not troubled by the notion of a cognitive response, but were only concerned by a visceral response to something 'filthy' and 'disgusting' (2001, p13).

On 9 November 1996, *The Daily Mail*'s front-page article was headlined 'Ban this car crash sex film' and included a quote from Virginia Bottomley urging 'local authorities to use the powers they have to refuse the film a screen. There is too much violence.' There were also negative quotes from Mary Whitehouse and two Conservative MPs, although there was no indication that they had actually seen the film. Also in this edition of the paper was an article by Christopher Tookey headlined 'Morality dies in the twisted wreckage', arguing that the film 'promulgates ... the morality of the satyr, the nymphomaniac, the rapist, the paedophile, the danger to society.' He proves his argument by referring to the fact that 'the initially heterosexual characters lose their inhibitions [and] they experiment pleasurably with gay sex, lesbian sex and sex with cripples' (Kermode and Petley, 1997, p16). This wildly over-determined rhetoric exemplifies the way in which moral panics depend upon a Manichean world view – there are only two positions available, either *for* or *against* that which threatens order. Significantly, for Tookey (and the *Mail*) order appears to be threatened by any variation in sexual practice – a revelation that if one accepts being recruited as a 'concerned individual' within this discourse, one is simultaneously being co-opted by a conservative, moralistic, right-wing agenda.

Barker et al (2001) refer to a subsequent article by Tookey in the *Mail* in which he argues that

> joy-riding, ram-raiding and reckless driving by the young are already social problems. Cronenberg's reputation as a cult horror director might tempt many more to seek out this movie than would normally be attracted to a boring, repetitious arthouse film.

Barker et al alert us to the poverty of the argument and Tookey's use of the 'full might of the random hypothetical' and we can also observe here that, in the maelstrom of the moral panic, the film is simultaneously cause, effect and symptom of cultural deterioration. In addition, we might ask that, if the 'many more' (presumably young potential deviants) who are tempted to seek out the film are then confronted with a 'boring, repetitious arthouse film', why this might be a problem? Won't they simply be bored?

The *Mail* used the film as a vehicle to attack liberalism and the 'intellectual establishment', most notably through an article by Bel Mooney on 30 November 1996 in which, despite only devoting two paragraphs to the film, she treats *Crash* as a symptom of a moral decline that must be halted, arguing:

> I am talking about the limits of freedom of expression. About whether we shall allow our society to be corrupted by a handful of people who believe that there are no boundaries to what the screen should show or the writer describe. Over many a dinner table I have argued that unless people like myself take a stand against the seemingly endless downward spiral of sex and violence in books, film and on television, the world that I was born into will disappear forever, and we shall allow our children to inherit a moral vacuum, not a civilised community. (Barker et al, 2001, p14)

We can identify here an implicit mobilisation of one of the tropes of the moral panic, the metaphor of disaster – the inexorable tide or landslide which threatens to engulf us unless something is done. The effectiveness of the trope is that it marks the threat as singular and the necessary response as simple. The article also exposes the right-wing conservative agenda of the *Mail* which, as it became increasingly isolated in its campaign against *Crash*, resorted to personal attacks on members of the BBFC, indicting them for coming from 'trendy arts and public-service backgrounds' (Kermode and Petley, 1997, p18).

Barker et al argue:

> The most striking thing in all the *Mail's* articles about *Crash* is the virtual absence of argument. Repeated tirades are packed with adjectives, and warnings of doom ... There is a total absence of evidence or argument in the *Mail's* coverage, a wholesale presence of moral screaming. (2001, p14)

This campaign against the film exemplifies the way in which a newspaper can claim the moral high ground and appoint itself crusader against a 'threat' to 'our' way of life by using powerful rhetoric. The *Mail* offered its readers the opportunity to ally themselves with this appealing, bold position while also providing entertainment in the form of 'salacious details' of that being condemned. Lurid headlines, explicit details, exaggeration and moral certitude are a potent combination and may, of course, sell more papers.

Case study 5: A debate in action – Forna vs Kermode

In 1999 Channel 4 broadcast a short season of programmes about censorship, as well as some controversial films. The season included two short programmes, one advocating censorship and one challenging it. In *Don't Look Now*, the writer, journalist and broadcaster Aminatta Forna makes the case for censorship. In *Eyes Wide Open*, the film critic and broadcaster Mark Kermode makes the case against. Their arguments are summarised below.

● *Don't Look Now*: A case for censorship (Aminatta Forna)

Forna begins by arguing that 'in the adult world of mass media and mass audiences we're beginning to recognise the power of words and images to harm'. As a writer she recognises the importance of freedom of expression, but also recognises that freedom comes with responsibilities.

> If my right threatens the freedom of others then it can't be an absolute right and since 1976 British laws have recognised that argument in terms of racial hatred. Allowing some groups to use their freedom to stir racial hatred removes the freedom of minorities to live without persecution.

Despite the fact that the Race Relations Act extends to film, argues Forna, the BBFC has passed uncut *Romper Stomper* (Geoffrey Wright, Australia, 1992), a film which

> follows the fortunes of a group of skinheads on a violent mission to keep their neighbourhood white. Scenes of racial violence are preceded by rousing music, giving the film the glamour of a pop video – it had all the makings of a cult movie. The film was crafted so that our interest lies with the skinheads – we hear their philosophy, understand their fears, engage with their lives and relationships, but the filmmaker chooses not to humanise their victims in the same way. I live only a few miles from where Stephen Lawrence was murdered. At a local market neo-Nazis militate on a Saturday morning. A while ago someone painted 'niggers out' on a house in my street. It's not difficult to imagine how *Romper Stomper*'s apparent endorsement of racial violence and white purity could translate into violence there. If the local cinema planned to give the film a two-week run I would want the council to use their powers its to prevent *Romper Stomper* being shown.

'But racism in the cinema', continues Forna, 'is hardly a new issue', describing *The Birth of a Nation* (D W Griffith, USA, 1915) as an

> unashamedly racist account of the turmoil at the end of the Civil War and the threat posed to a Southern town by newly emancipated blacks. Griffith knew which levers to pull to rouse his white audiences – there are three separate instances of black men coveting, molesting and attempting to rape white women. In America in the first half of this century thousands of black men were lynched, often for the 'crime' of looking at a white woman. We don't know if Griffith's film was responsible for any single attack, but he went out of his way to advocate lynching in the film and if one black man died in that way as a result I would have wanted to see him prosecuted. At the finale the Ku Klux Klan ride to the rescue in scenes which it's said drove audiences into a frenzy; I would not have liked to be a black man passing the cinema as the crowds spilled out.

Addressing the view that *The Birth of a Nation*'s artistry is more important than its message, Forna argues that:

> It remains immaterial – is a beautifully directed snuff movie or Hitler's rhetoric mitigated because they both demonstrate considerable artistic flair? Of course not. Nowadays *Birth of a Nation* looks dated, but at that time it was the craftsmanship itself that made the film's message so effective and so deadly,

the proof of this being that the Ku Klux Klan used a poster featuring a still from the film (of a Klan member on a triumphantly rearing horse) for recruitment purposes.

Turning her attention to the general potency of images, Forna says:

> Images have the power to create desires – advertisers know that to the tune of billions. TV ads today make use of cinema's narrative devices, but when we see an advert we know we're being sold something; when we watch a movie we don't employ the same defences. In the cinema product placement sells watches, cameras, clothes to us in the course of an action movie – it works because we associate ourselves with the characters. Triggers in our brain connect with what we're seeing – ask any smoker who's watched Bogart or Bacall draw on a cigarette and reached for the pack themselves. Desires are created and acted upon, whether or not that's what the filmmaker expressly intended. Experience has shown that when suicides are shown on TV there'll be an increase in attempts that night. One episode of *EastEnders* in which the character Angie tried to kill herself was thought to have prompted a country-wide series of emergencies that same evening.

Regarding sexual violence, Forna suggests that:

> Laws exist to deter us from doing what we might otherwise be tempted to do, after all something no one desires to do scarcely requires a law forbidding it. A society decides to censure certain acts, for example rape or sex with minors, precisely because the temptation is there and, despite the scepticism of critics, there's no shortage of research connecting visual images to sexual violence.

Commenting on an extract from the rape scene in *Straw Dogs*, Forna argues that:

> A male viewer who finds himself becoming aroused by the rape in this scene is also shown a woman becoming orgasmic moments after being beaten up – so a woman enjoys it in the end – 'no' does in fact mean 'yes'. What prevents a man who fantasises about rape from committing such an act are his own personal inhibitions as well as social inhibitions against it. Scenes like this repeated often enough start to destroy those barriers. No one's claiming that film is the only cause, but it's part of it, and in my opinion the scene should have been cut.

Forna accuses *Perdita Durango* (Alex De La Iglesia, Spain/Mexico, 1997) of fuelling similar fantasies, explaining that

> An hour of adrenaline surging violence climaxes in a rape. The rape arouses those in the film and is designed to arouse the viewer. But the director allays the spectator's guilty pleasures by suggesting that the woman enjoys the attack. In fact, before giving Perdita Durango a certificate the BBFC insisted that the rape scene be cut to remove, firstly shots that served to titillate the audience and secondly the suggestion that the woman took pleasure in being raped, I think once again quite rightly.

Saying films should be cut or not even shown is never going to be a popular position to hold. People who say that are accused of being prudes at best and, at worst, philistines. But then no one can argue for art or freedom of expression more convincingly than a director with his cut of the box office. Setting limits to what can be shown to mass audiences is part of the responsibility of living in a sophisticated democracy. Films aren't lives and directors and their art aren't above mere mortals. Some people say that adults should be allowed to see anything so long as it wasn't actually illegal in the making. Well think about this – with new digital imaging techniques I could make films of adults having sex with children – it would look absolutely convincing. One day soon you won't even be able to tell that the children aren't real and since no actual children would be involved there wouldn't be any harm in it all, right? Or perhaps not. The fact is images and words have the power to distort the way we think – they can promote racial violence or lead to sexual aggression. The existing law does what it can to protect people because in reality society isn't divided neatly into deviants and the rest of us. The truth lies in recognising the beast within us all and setting a framework for human decency. (*Don't Look Now*, 1999)

● *Eyes Wide Open*: A case against censorship (Mark Kermode)

Kermode begins his argument (the programme pre-dates the video releases of *I Spit on Your Grave*, *Straw Dogs* and *The Driller Killer*) with the provocation:

> You are an idiot; you are stupid, weak, impressionable, easily led and unable to distinguish between fiction and reality. If you're an adult you're probably an immature one and if you're a parent you're a very bad one. I, on the other hand, am intelligent, culturally sophisticated, parentally adept and able to appreciate art and eager to prevent you from attempting to do the same thing because, frankly, you're just not up to the job. In short I know what's good for you and you don't. Now put like that it all sounds rather unpleasant doesn't it, but that's exactly what Britain's film censors are saying to you every day of the week. As a result you can't currently watch movies like *Straw Dogs* or *Driller Killer* in your living room, the seminal shocker *The Evil Dead* is a couple of minutes shorter than it ought to be, wherever you see it; *Henry: Portrait of a Serial Killer* has got some of its scenes put back to front so they don't make sense any more and people in sex films don't actually have sex. It's also why *Bad Lieutenant* … isn't quite so bad.

Kermode argues that

> The basis for all this madness is a peculiarly British fear of freedom and responsibility, a fear which is best expressed in the much lauded Obscene Publications Act which outlaws material demonstrating a tendency to deprave or corrupt a significant proportion of its likely audience. Supporters of the OPA applaud the fact that it considers works of art as

a whole, examining each element in context and asking what effect does the work in its entirety have upon its audience.

The BBFC has a duty to cut or ban any film or video which might fall foul of this law, but 'that's not as simple as it sounds because obviously the law is open to wide interpretation'. This is illustrated by the fact that (then BBFC director) James Ferman was publicly chastised by Jack Straw, the Home Secretary at the time, for passing the sex work *Batbabe*, which was subsequently impounded by Customs and Excise for being 'obscene'. Kermode comments ironically that

> Apparently Ferman had decided that in the 90s the sight of adults indulging in mutually pleasurable sex was not likely to deprave or corrupt the clientele of licensed sex shops; to him modern porn videos like this were far less troublesome than say age old 'problem films' like *I Spit on Your Grave*, a violent thriller which depicts lengthy gang rapes shot with gritty realism.

Kermode imagines that many Channel 4 viewers would agree with Ferman in being happy to legalise consensual porn but wanting to suppress some more violent material, and points out that *I Spit on Your Grave* has 'long been outlawed in the UK under the terms of the OPA because it allegedly encourages the viewer to revel in the pain and degradation of a woman.' Raising the question of just how vile this film is, Kermode refers us to Marco Starr's essay in *The Video Nasties*, which argues that the film can be read as a 'feminist tract', 'presenting the heroine's suffering not as titillation, but as an unbearable ordeal for the audience, as indeed it should be'. Kermode says he's met many fans of exploitation cinema who hated *I Spit on Your Grave* because 'It wasn't any fun at all to watch. It appalled them, but it didn't corrupt them.'

He adds that he personally loathes Lars Von Trier's *Breaking the Waves* because it delights

> in the spectacle of a nubile child woman enduring endless rounds of sexual humiliation – by having to masturbate an aged stranger on a bus – all in the service of her husband and all deemed to be OK because at the end of the movie she gets to go to heaven. Now I think this is really pernicious misogynistic stuff, but that isn't how it plays to the film's numerous fans – men and women – who apparently find it moving and uplifting. Nor to the BBFC who passed it uncut on film and video. So why do these films inspire such polarised and opposite reactions? The answer is that although we may all watch the same film we see different films – films that are as individual as our own personal responses to them, and it's this that makes the practice of film censorship a nonsense. It's one thing for critics to argue amongst themselves about the relative virtues of *Crash*, but it's quite another when our censors cut two minutes of zombies clawing at bloody wounds out of the 18-rated *Evil Dead* in the belief that this will somehow make it less likely to deprave and corrupt.

Kermode draws attention to the fact that under the terms of the Video Recordings Act all videos, even those rated for adults, are cut to make them suitable for viewing in the home, that is, safe for children who might surreptitiously access them when their parents aren't looking. He argues that 'This is the equivalent of watering down all alcohol available in off licences on the basis that you might be a lousy parent who allows kids open access to the drinks cabinet.' He adds that this of course does no good – even in its cut form *The Evil Dead* is still going to upset children ('whose parents can't be bothered to monitor their viewing habits').

Kermode goes on to indict the BBFC for not just cutting and diluting, but also because 'when the mood takes them they actually like to change the meaning of movies too.' He refers us to a scene from John McNaughton's *Henry: Portrait of a Serial Killer* in which the director wanted to implicate the audience in the killers' voyeurism by refusing to devolve the gaze (at a video of the murder of a family in their own home) onto the characters within the scene, but the BBFC was unhappy with this and inserted some reaction shots of Henry and his accomplice watching their handiwork, thus changing the impact of the scene.

Kermode asks:

> So where does this all stop? Should we re-edit ... *The Birth of a Nation* so that it no longer glorifies the Ku Klux Klan? Should we ban *Romper Stomper* ... because some anti-Nazi organisations think it incites racial violence? Or should we accept as George Orwell did, that if freedom of speech is to mean anything it must be the freedom for people to say things which we don't want to hear. Well that's what I think, but it's very hard to maintain freedom of speech in a culture which has become terminally infantilised. We've allowed the censors to view us all as children and we've handed over the reins of responsibility for our viewing habits because we're not willing to accept that responsibility for ourselves. We've invited Big Brother into our homes and begged him to look after us and our kids. But of course he can't; films and videos cannot be made safe for everyone.

> The horror writer Ramsey Campbell once reported that the most frightening thing he'd ever seen was the image of a walking tree in a *Rupert the Bear* annual, which had caused him months of nightmares. Every year children are reduced to floods of tears by the death of Bambi's mother in a scene which has haunted generations. Even though she dies off screen, the story is so strong and this scene so powerful that many viewers believe they've witnessed something far more explicit than what is actually shown. The truth is that no matter what our censors do, art and literature will continue to inspire strange and baffling responses in people and the removal of a few seconds from a movie here or the re-editing of a video there won't do anything except create a climate in which censorship is erroneously considered to be a valid and necessary operation.

Kermode offers this three-part solution:

1. We need to accept the fact that the idea of policing the effect of movies at some kind of national level is impossible.

2. We need to need to get beyond the idea of obscenity and accept that there really is no such thing as a provable tendency to deprave and corrupt.

3. The BBFC should restrict itself to classifying and describing material, making cuts only when an actual offence has been committed in the *production* of the movie. This is the one area in which British censors are ahead of the world. Kermode argues:

    > This is the legitimate face of film policing because it concentrates not on the indefinable subject of what a film means to its audience, but on the concrete factual issue of what that film did to its participants. But beyond that we need to stop cutting and banning movies intended for adults, we need to seriously rethink our attitude about whose job it is to protect our children, we need to stop pretending that these are decisions that someone else can make for us and we need to open our eyes to the possibility of a future free from censorship.

Worksheet 16 asks students to summarise these arguments in order to have a record of clearly defined pro- and anti-censorship arguments. It is worth pointing out that, in the intervening years, *I Spit on Your Grave* and *The Driller Killer* have both been given video certificates, albeit in cut forms, but that videos are still treated much more strictly than films by the Board.

To access student worksheets and other online materials go to *Teaching Film Censorship and Controversy* at **www.bfi.org.uk/tfms** and enter User name: **filmcens@bfi.org.uk** and Password: **te1908ce**.

1 of 2 pages

This is a useful exercise in identifying, selecting and prioritising and can be followed up by some informal dialogue between group members. If appropriate, and if opinion seems to be fairly evenly divided, it might be possible to set up a formal debate in the classroom with teacher or confident student in the role of chair. The chair's job will be to ensure that points and evidence are clearly articulated and reiterated and that 'common-sense' assertions do not go unchallenged. It might be useful to challenge Forna's comparison of the meanings and effects of advertising with the meanings and effects of violent films. It might also be useful to examine Kermode's simile of 'watering down alcohol'. In any case, having done even some of the reading and exercises in this guide, it is likely that students will feel able to engage confidently with the different arguments.

Glossary

Several of these terms do not appear in this book, but provide useful additional background information in discussions of film censorship. This glossary is also available as a student handout at www.bfi.org.uk/tfms.

BBFC
The British Board of Film Classification – the body responsible for classifying films, videos, DVDs and digital games in the UK. It is an independent, non-government body funded by the fees it charges to those who submit work for classification. It has complete control (and statutory responsibilities) over video classification and censorship, but has less power regarding theatrical releases; it classifies films on behalf of local authorities, but local authorities still have the power to reject a BBFC decision about a particular film.

BVA
The British Video Association. This trade organisation represents the interests of video distributors and rights owners and so is particularly geared to licensing and piracy issues.

Censorship
The suppression of information, images, words etc on the grounds that they are damaging in some way to all or part of society.

Effects theory
An interpretation of the relationship between the media and its audience predicated on the notion that a certain kind of quantifiable input results in a certain kind of measurable output.

Hypodermic needle model
A metaphor for the 'stimulus-response' model of communication in which a syringe is analogous to the media and the 'drug' it carries represents media messages. (See effects theory.)

Libertarianism
A philosophical principle founded on the notion that human beings require absolute freedom of thought and expression.

Male gaze

A theory of film spectatorship derived from psychoanalysis and formalised by Laura Mulvey in her essay, 'Visual Pleasure and Narrative Cinema', originally published in *Screen* in 1975. Mulvey argues that film reproduces the sexual imbalance that obtains in real life by objectifying female characters and presenting them as spectacle. Thus the 'gaze' of the film is inherently masculine.

Mediawatch-UK

Formerly the National Viewers' and Listeners' Association, founded by Mary Whitehouse in 1965. Mediawatch-UK describes itself as providing an independent voice for those concerned about issues of taste and decency in the media. It lobbies for stricter controls on representations of sex, violence and swearing in the media as well as for more positive representations of marriage and family life.

Moral panic

A term coined by Stanley Cohen in *Folk Devils and Moral Panics*, first published in 1972. He defines it as an episode in which society is subjected to anxiety about a perceived threat to its values, interests and principles. The condition of 'moral panic' can be produced by areas of the media which may identify and amplify supposed 'deviations' from society's norms and present them as a serious threat to the nation's stability.

National Viewers' and Listeners' Association (NVLA)

See Mediawatch-UK

Ofcom

The Office of Communications – the regulator for the media and telecommunications industries. Launched at the end of 2003, it replaced five bodies: the Independent Television Commission, the Broadcasting Standards Commission, the Radio Authority, the Radiocommunications Agency and Oftel. Ofcom regulates standards of taste and decency on all TV and radio channels. It also licenses commercial TV and radio.

Obscenity

Notoriously difficult to pin down, but the definition in the Obscene Publications Act is still legally valid; if a work has a tendency to deprave and corrupt it is classed as obscene. What this actually means is fiercely contested.

Paternalism

Refers to the way in which a governing body restricts the freedoms of its 'subjects' in order to protect them. Paternalistic practices treat the recipients like children and are justified on the grounds that what is being done is 'for their own good'.

Polysemy

Plurality of meaning. Polysemic texts or elements within texts are ambiguous and open to a variety of interpretations. Arguably polysemy is a constant state and meaning is only ever contingent – dependent upon contextual factors and 'anchored' in a fluid way rather than fixed.

Psychoanalytic theory

This looks for meaning in texts by relating the events, character relations and modes of representation to the formation of the individual psyche in Western culture. Drawing on the work of Freud and Lacan, psychoanalytical approaches to textual analysis identify patterns and points of audience identification which may evoke, for example, common traumatic childhood experiences or castration anxiety.

Public interest

A distinction can be made between that which is *in* the public interest and that which is simply *of* public interest. Controversial material is often defended on the grounds that it serves to inform and educate about serious issues and it is, therefore, *in* the public interest that it is seen/heard/read. Alternatively, moral panics whipped up by the press, often paying scant regard to logic and factual evidence, will often use 'public interest' as a justification.

Realism

A mode of representation, dependent upon technical and performance characteristics, which encourages suspension of disbelief in the viewer. Realism will be constructed in different ways depending upon the genre of the work. Censorship decisions regarding violence are often related to the realism of the text; something may be justified because it is 'realistic' and somehow 'responsible' but, alternatively (and perhaps contradictorily), arguments may be founded on the fact that action is presented as fantasy and is therefore 'harmless'.

Stereotype

Highly selective, over-simplified, often negative representation of a social group or individual. Stereotypes are frequently invoked as a 'common-sense' shorthand in debates about film censorship in order to argue that a particular social group may be, for example, prone to violence, particularly vulnerable or incompetent/negligent.

Uses and gratifications theory

An alternative to effects theory which focuses on how and why people may use the media, rather than on particular types of content. Whereas effects theory constructs the audience as homogeneous and essentially passive, Uses and gratifications theory posits a heterogeneous audience with a wide range of possible interactions with media texts.

Voyeurism

Often used synonymously with the term 'scopophilia', voyeurism is predicated on the concept of a subject (usually male) gaining sexual satisfaction from watching an objectified Other.

VPRC

The Video Packaging Review Committee, administered by the BBFC, but attended by industry representatives. This was introduced in 1987 and is a voluntary system designed to prevent offence to members of the public caused by explicitly violent or sexual imagery on the covers of video cassettes.

VSC

The Video Standards Council. A voluntary trade association representing the whole of the video and games industries and designed to encourage good practice and promote high standards. It has no statutory power.

Watershed

On terrestrial television a turning point in the evening's schedule which occurs at 9pm. Before this time there is a tacit understanding that broadcasters will ensure that viewing is suitable for children; after this time the responsibility lies with parents to regulate children's viewing.

References and resources

Filmography

9 Songs (Michael Winterbottom, UK, 2004)
L'Arrivée d'un train en gare de la ciotat (Lumière Brothers, France, 1895)
Bad Lieutenant (Abel Ferrara, USA, 1992)
Baise-moi (Virginie Despentes/Coralie Trinh Thi, France, 2000)
The Battleship Potemkin (Sergei Eisenstein, USSR, 1925)
The Birth of a Nation (D W Griffith, USA, 1915)
Blow-Up (Michaelangelo Antonioni, UK/Italy, 1966)
Boyz N the Hood (John Singleton, USA, 1991)
Breaking the Waves (Lars Von Trier, Denmark/Sweden/France/Netherlands, 1996)
Cannibal Holocaust (Ruggero Deodato, USA, 1980)
Un Chien andalou (Luis Buñuel and Salvador Dali, France, 1928)
Child's Play 3 (Jack Bender, USA, 1991)
A Clockwork Orange (Stanley Kubrick, UK, 1971)
Crash (David Cronenberg, Canada, 1996)
Die Hard (John McTiernan, USA, 1988)
The Driller Killer (Abel Ferrara, USA, 1979)
The Evil Dead (Sam Raimi, USA, 1981)
The Exorcist (William Friedkin, USA, 1974)
Festen (Thomas Vinterberg, Denmark, 1998)
Fight Club (David Fincher, USA, 1999)
Frankenstein (James Whale, USA, 1931)
Funny Games (Michael Haneke, Austria, 1997)
La Haine (Mathieu Kassovitz, France, 1995)
Halloween (John Carpenter, USA, 1978)
Happiness (Todd Solondz, USA, 1998)
Henry: Portrait of a Serial Killer (John McNaughton, USA, 1986)
I Spit on Your Grave (Meir Zarchi, USA, 1978)
If.... (Lindsay Anderson, UK, 1968)

In the Company of Men (Neil LaBute, USA, 1997)

Intimacy (Patrice Chéreau, UK/France, 2001)

Irreversible (Gaspar Noé, France, 2002)

Juice (Ernest Dickerson, USA, 1992)

Killing Zoe (Roger Avary, France/USA, 1994)

Lara Croft: Tomb Raider (Simon West, USA/Germany/UK/Japan, 2001)

The Last House on the Left (Wes Craven, USA, 1972)

Last Tango in Paris (Bernardo Bertolucci, France/Italy, 1972)

The Last Temptation of Christ (Martin Scorsese, USA/Canada, 1988)

Man Bites Dog (Remy Belvaux/André Bonzel/Benoit Poelvoorde, Belgium, 1992)

The Matrix (Andy Wachowski/Larry Wachowski, USA/Australia, 1999)

Monty Python's Life of Brian (Terry Jones, UK, 1979)

My Name Is Joe (Ken Loach, UK/Germany, 1998)

Natural Born Killers (Oliver Stone, USA, 1994)

Out for Justice (John Flynn, USA, 1991)

The Passion of the Christ (Mel Gibson, USA, 2004)

Perdita Durango (Alex De La Iglesia, Spain/Mexico, 1997)

Pink Flamingos (John Waters, USA, 1972)

Platoon (Oliver Stone, USA, 1986)

Psycho (Alfred Hitchcock, USA, 1960)

Pulp Fiction (Quentin Tarantino, USA, 1994)

Rambo: First Blood 2 (George Pan Cosmatos, USA, 1985)

Reservoir Dogs (Quentin Tarantino, USA, 1992)

Romance (Catherine Breillat, France, 1999)

Romper Stomper (Geoffrey Wright, Australia, 1992)

A Room for Romeo Brass (Shane Meadows, UK/Canada, 1999)

Saló (Pier Paolo Pasolini, Italy/France, 1975)

Schindler's List (Steven Spielberg, USA, 1993)

Seul contre tous (Gaspar Noé, France, 1998)

Spider-Man (Sam Raimi, USA, 2002)

The Spy Who Loved Me (Lewis Gilbert, UK, 1977)

Straw Dogs (Sam Peckinpah, UK, 1971)

Sunday, Bloody Sunday (John Schlesinger, UK, 1971)

Sweet Sixteen (Ken Loach, UK/Germany/Spain/France/Italy, 2002)

The Texas Chainsaw Massacre (Tobe Hooper, USA, 1974)

True Romance (Tony Scott, USA, 1993)

Visions of Ecstasy (Nigel Wingrove, UK, 1989)

The War Zone (Tim Roth, UK/Italy, 1998)

Who's Afraid of Virginia Woolf? (Mike Nichols, USA, 1966)

The Wild One (Laslo Benedek, USA, 1953)

Women in Love (Ken Russell, UK, 1969)

Bibliography

A Akwagyiram, 2003, 'Howells Attacks Screen Violence', *The Guardian*, 13 January

N Andrews, 1984, 'Nightmares and Nasties', in M Barker (ed), *The Video Nasties: Freedom and Censorship in the Media*, Pluto Press, pp39–47

M Barker (ed), 1984, *The Video Nasties: Freedom and Censorship in the Media*, Pluto Press

M Barker, 1993, 'Sex, Violence and Videotape', in *Sight and Sound*, vol 3, no 5, May, pp10–12

M Barker, 1997, 'The Newson Report: A Case Study in "Common Sense"', in M Barker and J Petley (eds), *Ill Effects: The Media/Violence Debate*, Routledge, pp12–31

M Barker, 2002, 'Categories of Violence', in *Media Magazine*, September, pp26–9

M Barker, 2004, 'Violence Redux', unpublished essay

M Barker, J Arthurs and R Harindranath, 2001, *The Crash Controversy: Censorship, Campaigns and Film Reception*, Wallflower Press

M Barker and J Petley (eds), 2001, *Ill Effects: The Media/Violence Debate* (2nd Ed), Routledge

BBC Online, 2002, 'Loach Urges Young to Defy Censors', at http://news.bbc.co.uk/1/hi/entertainment/film/2298449.stm

D Buckingham, 1993, 'Boys' Talk: Television and the Policing of Masculinity', in *Reading Audiences: Young People and the Media*, Manchester University Press, pp89–115

Censored, 1999, BBC Radio 4, 3 January [Radio off-air recording]

C J Clover, 1992, *Men, Women and Chainsaws: Gender in the Modern Horror Film*, bfi

G Cumberbatch, 2002, *Where Do You Draw the Line? Attitudes and Reactions of Video Renters to Sexual Violence in Film*, BBFC, at http://www.bbfc.co.uk/website/Downloads.nsf/de40125acfd0b28a80256cb b004d6ad1/$FILE/Where_do_you_draw_the_line.pdf

T Dewe Matthews, 1994, *Censored*, Chatto and Windus

Dispatches: Video Game Violence and Children, 2000, Channel 4, 23 March [TV off-air recording]

Don't Look Now, 1999, Channel 4, 20 February [TV off-air recording]

R Falcon, 1994, *Classified!: A Teachers' Guide to Film and Video Censorship and Classification*, bfi

R Falcon, 1998, 'The Discreet Harm of the Bourgeoisie', *Sight and Sound*, vol 8, no 5, May, pp10–12

R Falcon, 1999, 'Reality Is Too Shocking' *Sight and Sound*, vol 9, no 1, January, pp10–13

L Felperin, 2003, *Irreversible* (Review), *Sight and Sound*, vol 13, no 3, March, pp46–8

S Garrett, 2002, 'Ambushing the Audience', *The Guardian*, 3 June

D Gauntlett, 2001, 'The Worrying Influence of "Media Effects", Studies' in M Barker and J Petley (eds), *Ill Effects: The Media/Violence Debate*, Routledge

B Gunter, 1998, *The Effects of Video Games on Children: The Myth Unmasked*, Sheffield Academic Press

C Hastings, 2004, 'This Will Open the Floodgates to Hardcore Porn', *Telegraph Online*, 24 October, at
www.telegraph.co.uk/news/main.jhtml;sessionid=1NEQM12S4HFZFQFIQM GSM5WAVCBQWJVC?view=HOME&grid=N1&menuId=-1&menuItemId=-1&_requestid=79416

A Hill, 1997, *Shocking Entertainment: Viewer Responses to Violent Movies*, John Libbey Media

N James and M Kermode, 2003, 'Horror Movie', *Sight and Sound*, vol 13, no 2, February, pp20–2

S Jeffries, 2005, 'I Am the Opposite of Ashamed', *The Guardian*, 24 January

T Johnston, 2001, 'Michael Haneke on *Funny Games*', *Funny Games*, Tartan Video [DVD extra]

C Kennedy, 2001, 'Hit That Perfect Beat Boy', *Empire*, March, pp84–7

M Kennedy, 2002, 'New Film Censor Keeps Cool Head', *The Guardian*, 2 August

M Kermode, 1997, 'I Was a Teenage Horror Fan: Or, How I Learned to Stop Worrying and Love Linda Blair', in M Barker and J Petley (eds), *Ill Effects: The Media/Violence Debate*, Routledge, pp57–68

M Kermode, 2001, 'Left on the Shelf', *Sight and Sound*, vol 11, no 7, July, p26

M Kermode and J Petley, 1997, 'Road Rage', *Sight and Sound*, vol 7, no 6, June, pp16–18

The Last Days of the Board, 1999, Channel 4, 20 February [TV off-air recording]

P Laverty, 2002, 'A Word with the Censors', *The Guardian*, 30 September

K Maher, 2003, 'What's Behind the Gore?', *The Observer*, 12 January

D Malcolm, 2004, 'Sex and the Cinema', *The Guardian*, 20 May

The Matrix *Defence*, 2003, Channel 4, 19 November [TV off-air recording]

D Miller and G Philo, 1996, 'Against Orthodoxy: The Media Do Influence Us', *Sight and Sound*, vol 6, issue 12, December, pp18–20

L Mulvey, 1992, 'Visual Pleasure and Narrative Cinema', in *The Sexual Subject: A* Screen *Reader in Sexuality*, Routledge, pp22–34

K Newman, 2001, 'The 10 Most Shocking Moments in Cinema History', *Empire*, March, pp88–9

Open Your Eyes, 1999, Channel 4, 21 February [TV off-air recording]

J Palmer, 1987, *The Logic of the Absurd*, bfi

Panorama: The Killing Screens, 1995, BBC1, 27 February [TV off-air recording]

G Pearson, 1984, 'Falling Standards: A Short Sharp History of Moral Decline', in M Barker (ed), *The Video Nasties: Freedom and Censorship in the Media*, Pluto Press, pp88–103

J Petley, 1997, 'Us and Them', in M Barker and J Petley (eds), *Ill Effects: The Media/Violence Debate*, Routledge, pp87–101

J Petley, 2001, 'Raising the Bar', *Sight and Sound*, vol 11, no 12, December, pp30–2

J Petley, 2002, 'Who Let the Dogs Out?' *Sight and Sound*, vol 12, no 12, December, p66

J Petley and M Kermode, 1998, 'The Censor and the State', *Sight and Sound*, vol 8, no 5, pp14–18

J Romney, 2001, '*Funny Games* Review', *Funny Games*, Tartan Video, [DVD extra]

M Starr, 1984, 'J. Hills Is Alive: A Defence of *I Spit on Your Grave*', in M Barker (ed), *The Video Nasties: Freedom and Censorship in the Media*, Pluto Press, pp48–55

A Travis, 2004, 'Film Censors to Survey Public Attitudes on Offensiveness of Swearing', *The Guardian*, 10 May

L R Williams, 1994, 'An Eye for an Eye', *Sight and Sound*, vol 4, no 4, April, pp14–16.

L R Williams, 2002, 'Less Rape, More Revenge', *Sight and Sound*, vol 12, no 4, 2002, p70

C Witchalls, 2004, 'Cruising for a Bruising', *Observer Magazine*, 15 February, p57

Further reading

P Church Gibson (ed), 2004, *More Dirty Looks: Gender, Pornography and Power*, bfi

P Holland, 1992, *What Is a Child?: Popular Images of Childhood*, Virago

D Kerekes and D Slater, 2000, *See No Evil: Banned Films and Video Controversy*, Critical Vision

A Kuhn, 1988, *Cinema, Censorship, and Sexuality, 1909–1925*, Routledge

J S Mill, 1974, *On Liberty*, Penguin

Useful websites

BBFC (www.bbfc.co.uk) – the site of the British Board of Film Classification with links to all of the classification guidelines, press releases and research documents

Censor Watch (www.censorwatch.co.uk/index.htm) – a 'censored' version of the Melon Farmers site (see below) in order to make it accessible via restricted search engines

Index on Censorship (www.indexonline.org) – linked with the magazine of the same title, Index on Censorship provides opinion, analysis and comment on freedom of expression issues. Film censorship is included, but there is more of an emphasis on political infringements of free speech

Mediawatch-uk (www.mediawatchuk.org) – a site dedicated to identifying and campaigning against 'harm and offence issues in the media'

Melon Farmers (www.melonfarmers.co.uk) – a site of 'news, information and opinion' relating to censorship which takes 'a particular interest in those that claim to occupy the moral high ground'

Ofcom (www.ofcom.org.uk) – the site of the regulator for UK communications industries which contains pdf files of broadcasting code guidance for TV

Screenonline (www.screenonline.org.uk/film/indaud.html) – the Industry and Audience section of the BFI's comprehensive guide to film and TV history. The censorship and legislation links provide access to case studies and legal issues.

An excellent source of video recordings of past TV programmes is: www.richmond-utcoll.ac.uk/facilities/video.asp

Acknowledgements

Thanks to: Vivienne Clark for her patience and advice; Pete Johnson for providing good answers to some not very good questions; Martin Barker for letting me have a copy of his unpublished essay 'Violence Redux'; my colleagues at Bridgwater College for intelligent conversation; and Helen for endurance.